START UP
FOREVER

Matador
9 Priory Business Park,
Wistow Road, Kibworth Beauchamp,
Leicestershire. LE8 0RX
Tel: 0116 279 2299
Email: books@troubador.co.uk
Web: www.troubador.co.uk/matador
Twitter: @matadorbooks

ISBN 978 1789016 345

British Library Cataloguing in Publication Data.
A catalogue record for this book is available from the British Library.

Printed and bound in Great Britain by 4edge Limited
Typeset in 12pt Janson by Troubador Publishing Ltd, Leicester, UK

Matador is an imprint of Troubador Publishing Ltd

"How do you encourage entrepreneurial behaviour in large organisations?

This is the problem to which Sahar Hashemi offers a straightforward solution. These lessons are easy to understand (there's no having to memorise complex management concepts)."

FINANCIAL TIMES
Business Book of the Month

Also by Sahar Hashemi:

Anyone Can Do It: Building Coffee Republic
From Our Kitchen Table

"Sahar Hashemi has a gift for storytelling. These pages radiate the warmth and humour with which she has passionately spoken so many times about her own experiences as an entrepreneur and subsequent conversations with 'big business'. There's an oversupply of frameworks and tools at the disposal of the 21st century 'intrapreneur', but this common-sense canter through 10 habits and no less than 34 small but significant 'shifts' is a well-crafted wake-up call to the dormant entrepreneur in all of us. Inspiring, human, humble. Just like the author."

Carl Nagel,
Global Marketing Innovation Director,
Jacobs Dowe Egberts

"This book is about how big companies learn more from smaller ones than vice versa; the biggest learning should be how to be big but entrepreneurial, in other words create an organisation that is driven by its own form of "intrepreneurship" … these are the companies that will win!"

Allan Leighton,
Chairman of The Co-operative Group,
Former CEO of Asda,
Chairman of Royal Mail

"A must read book to help managers reflect upon and leverage their state of mind. Sahar Hashemi succeeds in reconciling the brain with the heart through common sense, thereby providing a toolkit to foster, build and maintain the entrepreneurial culture which established big companies need to survive in today's world."

Bob Kunze-Concewitz,
CEO of Campari Group

"I still remember the impact of Sahar's speech at the LinkedIn Talent Connect London a few years ago – her story on creating an entrepreneurial mindset in large companies resonated with our audience and I am glad those tips are now turned into a book."

Carole Zibi,
Marketing Director, Linked In

"This is a wonderful book, full of ideas and practical tips on how to make the big established firm more entrepreneurial and innovative. It belongs on the shelf of all managers working in big firms."

Costas Markides,
Professor of Strategy and Entrepreneurship,
London Business School

"Sahar is a powerful catalyst to drive entrepreneurship within big corporations. This is not an easy topic, the risk of staying at theory level is high. The reason why I am actively endorsing Sahar is because she provided me and my organization with tangible tools to start making changes immediately. Her personal story is genuine, down to earth, super inspiring and extremely interesting to follow. She talks to people's heart in a way that awakens the entrepreneur inside. She sells a mindset and she equips you to go make it happen. Her deep experience with corporations makes her suggestions and her collection for do's and dont's very actionable. She does not provide theory and that's it. She is a change agent, a catalyst of change to drive entrepreneurship with a tangible and ready to use approach."

Stefano Volpetti,
Vice President, Proctor & Gamble

"So many business books are as tedious as they are thick. Thankfully, Sahar Hashemi's Start Up Forever is short, snackable & filled with commonsense"

\sifted/ ▪

CONTENTS

BB [Big Business] **n.** an organisation of any size in any sector or industry showing symptoms of silo mentality, complexity, slowness, insularity and resistance to change.

PREFACE

This book is about how to think and behave like a start-up when you're not a start-up. It's my very straightforward and simple answer to the hotly debated and often complicated question of how to encourage entrepreneurial behaviour in large organisations. It has evolved out of my own personal experiences – my early corporate career, my start-up history, the 400 or so big organisations I have spoken to on this very topic and my immersion over these last twenty years in the entrepreneurial ecosystem – which have given me a thorough, ground-level understanding of what start-up culture really is and why it gets blocked in big companies. So before you begin this book, I need to tell you my story.

The truth is, I never thought in a million years that I would ever be an entrepreneur. Being brought up into the world of work and choosing my career in the 80s, entrepreneurship was the exclusive preserve of one man: first name, Richard. You can guess the rest. So, the role model who signified that particular career choice in my formative years was miles away from who I was. I hadn't set up a business in the kindergarten playground, hadn't made any money selling anything to anyone, hadn't shown one ounce of creative or leadership flair, and most importantly, I hadn't dropped out of school. My teachers would have no recollection of my talents. In fact, they would have no recollection of my existence at all. I was extremely ordinary. A mini Richard Branson in the making, I was clearly not. Nor was my brother Bobby.

We went down conventional, safe (and uncreative) routes. He became a banker and I a lawyer. But after the sudden death of our father, one thing led to another, and we jumped ship from our 'safe' careers and ended up looking for something to do. That's when we came across new-style US coffee bars in New York and decided to bring them to London.

Five years and 110 coffee bars later, with the *Financial Times* recognising us as a defining 'new Britain' brand, we got those incredibly unlikely – for a lawyer and a banker – new labels. We were officially known as (*drum-roll...*) entrepreneurs.

But just as we began to embrace this new status, the company we started, the one that had given us these exciting new careers as entrepreneurs, was losing its start-up label. Like a child growing up, it was getting big, becoming an adult. There was an industry boom and the UK was 'waking up to smell the coffee' (to recreate the headlines of many of the articles written about us). The sheer volume and numbers involved meant the company could no longer operate like the start-up we had built from our mum's kitchen table. We had thousands of employees and a market cap of £30m. Coffee Republic had to have proper management structure. It had to think and behave like a proper big business. A BB, as I shall call them from now on, with all the systems and controls that come with it.

I found it ironic at the time – and still do – that as we, personally, were being transformed into entrepreneurs, our start-up was being transformed into a typical BB.

The transformation felt like it happened almost overnight. One day we were a small, tight, flexible, informal, and disparate team, with no job titles, where everyone did everything, and our culture was the sum total of all our personalities glued together by our passion for the brand we were growing together, one day at a time. The next minute – and it really did seem that sudden – we got a new, high-flying MD who brought with him a whole equally high-flying team (none of whom would have ever considered working for us when we were a mere fledging start-up). And there it was, a flat-pack management culture ready to install. I know logically it didn't really happen overnight, but in my mind, I remember them stampeding in, immediately putting controls and systems and training manuals into place, and establishing formal lines of communication. There were clear delineations of roles and responsibilities, with almost no flexibility between each. It was almost as if, suddenly, high, impenetrable barriers went up around each person's desk. If one could physically see a silo forming, it was going up right before my eyes.

Just as suddenly as the management changed, the culture changed, too. Before, our guiding light was looking at everything from the customers' point of view. It was all about the bars and the customers' world, trying things out and not knowing, but just going for it. Now it was all about what was happening in the office: meetings, reviews, and formal procedures.

I found all these changes very difficult. Bobby and I decided it was time for us to leave the company. The start-up phase was over and, with that, so was the life span of us as entrepreneurs. We thought we had reached our sell-by date – that the company we had started no longer needed us. Like a child becoming an adult, we had to let go.

But letting go wasn't as easy and jubilant as we thought it would be. No one had warned us that leaving the company we had started and loved would be so painful. Instead of a celebration, it felt much more like a bereavement. When we removed Coffee Republic from our lives, we created a gaping hole, an emptiness where something that was not just a livelihood, but also such a source of passion and fulfilment, used to be.

To make it worse, in the years that followed, my brother and I were forced to watch from the sidelines as the company we had founded declined. By that time, Starbucks had really stepped up its UK expansion, and the new team, despite their strong CVs, didn't have what was needed to succeed in what was becoming a highly competitive market. The share price started to drop and now, as customers, we watched the brand we so loved become neglected. It is now just a shadow of its former self, which is obviously incredibly painful for us as founders.

But, as a change in circumstances often does, this painful transition got me started on a new journey. Someone suggested I write a book about our five-and-a-half-year experience. My initial reaction was resistance – I could hardly muster a thank you letter, let alone an entire book, but I started writing anyway. Following what you will soon learn is my typical *modus operandi*, I bought a book called *How to Write a Non-Fiction Bestseller* and followed the instructions therein. My first draft was around twenty pages long. I remember giving it to my long-suffering but ever-positive mother and telling her that was all I had. In typically encouraging fashion, she got me to delve deeper and deeper, and I found a pattern in the chaos of our whirlwind journey. That pattern was entrepreneurship.

I found that the steps we had taken were not unique in any way. I learnt that all entrepreneurs essentially make the same journey. The process of turning an ephemeral idea into reality puts everyone on the same course. You use the same behaviours. You use the same toolkit. Which is why I called my first book *Anyone Can Do It*, meaning exactly that, anyone *can* do it. *Anyone* can be an entrepreneur.

It's not about a particular personality or skill set. Entrepreneurship is a process anyone can follow, a step-by-step methodology that takes you from idea to reality. Once you take the leap, you start behaving entrepreneurially, quite unconsciously, as we did.

I found writing the book, sharing the warts-and-all breakthroughs and breakdowns, our thoughts, midnight ramblings and draft doodles, very cathartic. It helped with my emotional healing to go back through it all, to read the faxes and the jottings and dissect the journey we had taken. But it was also instructive. It was fascinating to learn that there was a method to the madness, as they say. It was also fulfilling to turn my experience into a real-life case study that demystified entrepreneurship, and to share it with all those who had a dream of starting a business but who, like us, were under the misconception that they lacked some kind of essential entrepreneur personality trait. That book went on to be a bestseller and inspire countless entrepreneurs, something of which I am very proud.

Then, two years after the book came out, there was a dramatic shift. Whereas immediately after it was released the audiences I spoke to were mostly aspiring entrepreneurs who needed motivation, and a story that would help them believe in themselves before taking the plunge, soon I started getting asked to speak at big companies about *my* story. To be honest, it was very uncomfortable at first – on both sides. On the company side, the joke I heard every time was, "Let's hope they don't all resign and start their own business after they've heard you!" The joke revealed the fear that, by demystifying entrepreneurship, I would encourage silently suffering employees to jump ship. From my side I, too, was hesitant. I had left the corporate world to move into the fun, connected, meaningful world of entrepreneurship. How could I gloss that over when the ethos of the corporate was so different to mine? How could I put a positive spin on working in the corporate world when it was so alien and so much less human than the exhilirating world where I had made my new home?

Quite quickly, the jokes about me being the catalyst for a wave of resignations dried up, and the agenda of every meeting with BB leadership became the same: change, and coping with change. Of course, change has been a constant since time immemorial. It is the pace of change that was shifting and necessitating new tools and approaches. Suddenly, companies that took a certain comfort in their size, scale, and market position were being threatened. Faster change was pushing companies out of their long-time comfort zones into the same choppy waters – full of uncertainty, shifting customer expectations, and scarce resources – that entrepreneurs have always operated in. But BBs don't know how to survive those waters. They are too set in their ways. Their sheer size and scale, which once gave them their biggest edge, has become their biggest liability. They can't manoeuvre quickly or keep up with the pace. They need to learn new ways of behaving, ways that are much more like how entrepreneurs have always done business, ways that are more agile, fluid, and lightweight.

That's why so many BBs wanted me to tell my story and to provide insight into what entrepreneurial behaviour means. And, for my part, I realised I was still demystifying entrepreneurship, but now for employees rather than for aspiring entrepreneurs. I was showing BBs how to navigate those choppy waters the same way entrepreneurs do, and in doing so, waking up BB employees to the possibilities and joys of the entrepreneurial mindset.

This book is the culmination of the approximately 400 talks I have given at big companies. Each time, I have gone over my own experiences and tried to distil the key behaviours that entrepreneurs do, and that big companies don't. The seeds of ideas that were planted with my experience at Coffee Republic, and grew as I sold my confectionary business, Skinny Candy, to a big conglomerate, have since fully matured during all the time I spent within those BBs.

I usually interact with companies when they have a planned, leadership meeting or conference, so rather than being bogged down in day-to-day considerations, leaders have been open and receptive to think big picture about their culture, and to set the tone for the year or years ahead. Watching this process unfold many times has given me amazing insight into the challenges that plague many BBs, and the ways in which they can move past them.

The solution that presents itself, again and again, isn't some giant reorganisation or top-down innovation initiative. Instead, it's simple shifts in mindset and behaviour that start with one person, or one team, and then spread around the business, building up big changes from many small tweaks. It's a few individuals thinking and acting more like entrepreneurs and, in doing so, showing just how powerful, do-able, and successful such behaviours can be. Then, step by step, almost by osmosis, these ways of working catch on. Most of this book is devoted to sharing and explaining those behaviour shifts.

But before we go into the behaviour shifts, I need to bust two big myths I encounter again and again when the phrase 'entrepreneurial behaviour' is mentioned in a BB. These myths create resistance to change, and they are not a million miles away from my own mindset at the beginning of my journey, so it's worth tackling them head on.

Myth 1: 'I am not an entrepreneur, or at all entrepreneurial.'

If it is challenging enough to demystify entrepreneurship for would-be entrepreneurs, it's even more challenging to do it for someone who has worked all of his or her life in a corporate environment. In the dictionary, the antonym of 'entrepreneur' is, believe it or not, 'employee'. No wonder so many employees feel that 'entrepreneurial in the corporate world' is as much of an oxymoron as a square circle, and worry they don't have what it takes to adopt these behaviours.

But the truth is that entrepreneurs and employees were never really opposites. They were never all that different from each other in terms of character or skills. The only difference is the context in which they have previously operated.

In the past, entrepreneurs and employees needed to behave in polar opposite ways because they operated in polar opposite environments. Employees were all about maintaining the status quo and executing tried-and-tested business models. Start-ups were – and are – about changing the status quo and finding new business models. The structures of the two types of business were totally opposite and that, naturally enough, resulted in opposing behaviours. Rigid employee behaviour was the direct result of rigid BB organisational structures. Free-flowing start-ups produced free-flowing, risk-taking entrepreneurs.

The good news for employees who believe they somehow lack what it takes to be entrepreneurial is that those structures have shifted. BBs need to not only innovate to survive in their markets, but also to become the sort of places that the new generation want to work for. These days BBs and start-ups are not very different from each other. Both are charged with innovation and keeping on top of a fast-changing market. Both need to find new business models to keep their businesses alive. And both need their people to behave in similar ways.

Starting a company has always pushed people, naturally, to activate certain traits and skills that are innate in all of us. Working at a BB, until now, hasn't done this, but that's changing. This new business environment will inevitably push employees to behave more like entrepreneurs – to make the sort of simple, intuitive shifts I outline in this book. You don't need some special personality. You don't need to be Steve Jobs or Mark Zuckerberg. You just need to be open to adopting straightforward new behaviours.

Myth 2: 'BBs can never have a start-up culture.'
I've lost count of the number of times I have heard this myth – that you can't change an entrenched corporate culture, or that BBs can never be entrepreneurial. Usually, when this belief comes up, the concept of the 'intrapreneur' comes up with it. In the 1970s, Gifford Pinchot coined the word to describe specific people charged with behaving like entrepreneurs within a big organisation. Many leaders I speak with still believe that being entrepreneurial is the job of some especially talented individual or team within the BB.

It was a valid idea in its time, but I want to move away from it. It implies that entrepreneurship is a specific, arcane speciality. It implies that it's not possible to shift the whole culture of an organisation, that a BB as a whole can never be entrepreneurial, and that you can never hope to expect entrepreneurialism from every employee. I think that's wrong, and Apple CEO Tim Cook agrees with me. *"A lot of companies have innovation departments, and this is always a sign that something is wrong,"* he has said. *"When you have a VP of Innovation, or something. You know, put a for sale sign on the door."*

This book is about the magic of bringing start-up culture to BBs in such a way that it infiltrates every department, every role – in short, every nook and cranny of a business. Of course, the road will not be as smooth as newly laid asphalt. There are always barriers, and set ways of doing things will have become entrenched and must be overcome. But knocking down these obstacles *is* possible, especially as there is so much latent talent ready to be tapped in BBs.

It takes a belief that culture is not static, that it is the sum total of individual behaviours. *The Lean Startup* author Eric Ries calls culture 'institutional muscle memory'. Change the behaviour and, over time, you develop new institutional muscle memory, also known as a new culture. First you start with your small team and then, slowly, the new ways of thinking and behaving spread to the whole organisation.

Companies who genuinely value fostering an entrepreneurial culture talk about 'vigilance' and 'counteracting their own complacency and default modes'. They fully recognise that they are not a kitchen table start-up, and they need systems and controls and that these, in a way, can oppose the spirit of entrepreneurialism. But because they understand this, they are proactive about balancing the need for organisation against the need for innovation. They think consciously about how to keep the necessary level of control without becoming bureaucratic, have processes without dehumanising employees, keep doing what works but still experiment, and use intuition but don't ignore research.

It's not easy, but it is possible, and I believe the rewards are huge. As they say, necessity is the mother of all invention, and right now BBs *need* to reinvent themselves. The shifting landscape of customer expectations and disrupt-or-die competition that keeps leaders of big organisations up at night also provides a golden opportunity to truly move culture away from habits left over from yesteryear, habits that every day become more out of step with the external world. New tools must replace that old-fashioned template, and start-up culture offers them. What could possibly be better than combining the agility of a start-up with the scale of a BB? What could possibly beat being the biggest small company in the world?

HOW TO USE THIS BOOK

In my work with BBs, I'm always asked the same questions:

- 'How can we grow big but act small?'
- 'How can we encourage innovative thinking and drive growth by finding different and new ways of doing things?'
- 'As we face disruptive change, how can we be more agile? More resilient? Less stuck in our ways?'
- 'How can I get my people to think outside the box, to experiment, and take the initiative?'
- 'How can I get everyone in the company to think more like *entrepreneurs?*'

The ten shifts in this book are my answers to these questions. I am not an innovation expert, with an elaborate system to expound, so there is no complicated methodology to learn. The solutions I have picked up on my journey are, in fact, strikingly common sense. They are simple shifts in how to approach everyday work with an entrepreneurial mind-set together with day-to-day actions anyone can take to put this more entrepreneurial mind-set to work.

Despite being so simple, these behaviours often get blocked in BBs. Ingrained behaviours that go back decades become automatic and push employees to keep mindlessly repeating habits from the past. This book is about introducing new habits to override those old, out-dated ones, unblocking people in BBs and freeing them to do things that come quite naturally to human beings when there are no institutional hurdles.

These habits are for everyone – no matter your role, job title or personal character. As I've explained, entrepreneurs aren't a different breed from employees. They are pushed to behave like entrepreneurs by the demands of starting a business. Old ideas operating in BBs have pushed employees to behave in other, less dynamic ways. By changing your mind-set and, through that, your behaviour, you can push back. Cultures aren't created by executive mandate. They accrete as the behaviours of individual employees, from assistants on up to executives, build up and calcify. Change your individual behaviour and you start to change the culture of your team and organisation. You also change your experience of going to work every day. Behaving like a entrepreneur is simply more fun and rewarding than being a cog in a corporate machine. These shifts build more innovative and successful businesses, but they also create happier, more engaged employees.

If I've done my job, you will see how one shift leads naturally on to the next. The shifts can be read independently of each other if you are pressed for time, but be aware they are interlocking and build on each other. 'Don't Depersonalise Customers', (#1), for instance, is the explanation of, and underpinning for, 'Don't Sit At Your Desk' (#2) while this second principle feeds back to boost empathy for customers in a virtuous cycle. This book is filled with these connections and feedback loops, so if at all possible, try to get through all the shifts for the greatest effect. Each one, if followed, will lead to set of practical actions you can implement immediately. Each gives you a new way to do your current job, rather than telling you to do entirely different things. Put together, the shifts form a blueprint for bringing a start-up mindset to your everyday work, and unleashing the potential to transform not just your sphere of influence but, the wider corporate culture, one person at a time.

"WE CAN'T BE ENTREPRENEURIAL BECAUSE..."

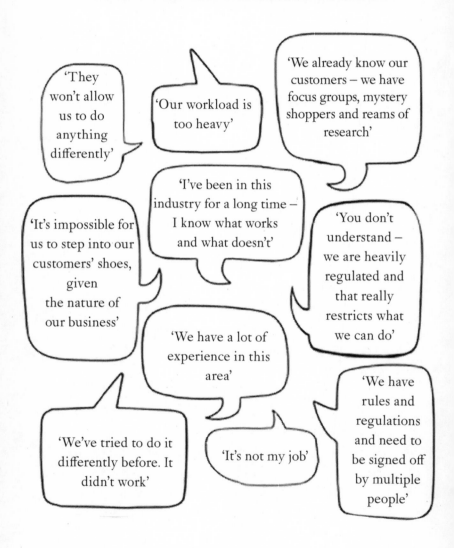

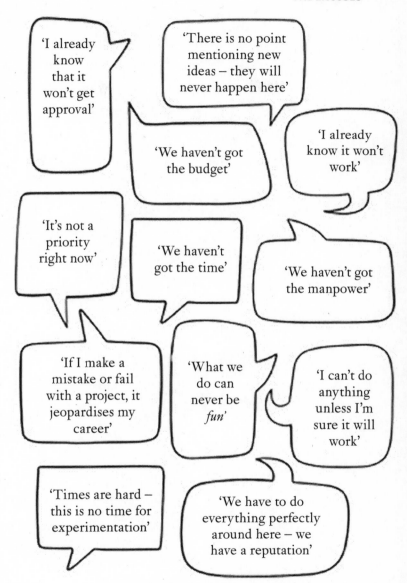

DO THESE EXCUSES SOUND FAMILIAR?

1

DON'T DEPERSONALISE CUSTOMERS

DO BECOME THEM INSTEAD

Turbo-charge empathy, it's the answer to everything

Empathy is the heart of this book. It's the source from which all the other behaviour shifts and day-to-day actions I discuss in this book spring. Empathy brings you into your customers' world and helps you see through their eyes, and once you get that right, everything flows naturally from there. So let me first explain the extraordinary power of empathy.

How well do you *really* know your customers?

Nearly every BB claims to be customer-centric. Saying, 'We love our customers!' – with a heart emoji next to the word 'customer' – is such a given it's a cliché. Ask any executive if customers are important and they'll instantly answer, *"Of course the customer is king! Customer service isn't a department, it's everyone's job..."* And so on. But I know from my own experience of being in both start-ups and in BBs that they have a completely different relationship with customers.

In BBs, customers end up on the outside because there's so much going on *inside* – a head office, structures, lines of reporting, targets to achieve, market share to worry about. By definition, the most important person is the person you report to: your boss. So customers inevitably come further down the list, and far away from the action. They become numbers and market segments rather than humans and they exist mainly within the remit of sales and marketing departments. In this way, BBs depersonalise customers. They become mythical, almost fictional.

At start-ups, however, the sun rises and sets with the customer. Getting a start-up off the ground is all about getting your first customers, and without them, there is simply no business. The supremacy of customers at the top the food chain is embedded in the culture, and in the mind, of the entrepreneur.

The 'kitchen table' character of the start-up also helps – there is no 'inside' to the business, no distractions or bureaucracy to keep people internally focused. There are no sales or customer service departments to whom customers can be fobbed off. Startups can't afford to pay for data and research about their customers. There is no data-driven 'archetypal customer'. So there is nothing coming between the entrepreneur and customer. Not only are customers *not* depersonalised but in fact, entrepreneur and customer are often one and the same.

It's probably no exaggeration to say that, in the vast majority of cases, entrepreneurs start out as their own customers. This was true for me. My brother and I started Coffee Republic because, as a tourist in New York, I came across skinny lattes and fat-free muffins in a new-style coffee bar called New World Coffee. When I returned home, I couldn't believe we didn't have them in London.

When I casually mentioned to my brother how much I missed the New York-style coffee bars, he had the mythical light bulb moment entrepreneurs are supposed to experience. "*That's it!*" he said. "*That is the business idea I've been looking for all my life,*" he carried on as I stared at him. "*You and I should be the ones to bring New York-style coffee bars to the UK.*"

"*Hang on a minute!*" I answered indignantly. "*I'm a customer. Why do I have to provide a solution to my own problem? Why doesn't someone else open it for me?*"

I know now what I didn't then: starting a business as the original customer is the strongest foundation possible. My brother and I built a business, in essence, so I could drink skinny lattes. And because I was not only the co-founder, but also the first customer, our 'market research' was simply putting ourselves in customers' shoes. All we had to do was ask, *"As a customer would I want this?"* (which was good, as we didn't have the money for market research anyway). It wasn't 'us' (the business) trying to sell something to 'them' (the customers). We *were* the customer.

This is not a unique story. So many of the innovations around us have started with an unmet personal need that was filled in a creative way. They start with the customer and work backwards. It's common sense, right? Sure, it's less obvious if you are working within the architecture of a large organisation, but it's still possible and just as important. Amazon, for example, 'obsesses over customers'. In the words of founder and CEO Jeff Bezos: *"We start with what the customer needs and work backwards."* This is a souped-up version of practicing day-to-day empathy in a BB. It's what we did as entrepreneurs, and what every BB should do: go back, and get as close to your customers as possible. Think what they think.

So, how can we translate this closeness – this way of relating to customers, of scratching your own itch– into an established BB when the product is already established, and customers are already out there, and, in a way, inherited? Of course, you can't suddenly 'become' your customer, so how do you find out what they want?

The answer is empathy. A *lot* of empathy.

Empathy isn't about being nice. It is the ability to share someone else's feelings or experiences by putting yourself in their shoes. It goes deeper than sympathy, which is more arm's length and objective. Empathy is about context – about thinking like the customer, experiencing the product through their eyes, as if you are in a virtual reality. It's very personal – we do it in our private life, reading the mood of our partner, predicting the feelings of our boss, or soothing our anxious child – but we are not used to doing it with customers. Empathy is a more human, intuitive, instinctive, subjective behaviour and, for that very reason, it can be difficult to achieve in large companies. Business is not meant to be personal, right? In a BB employees often feel they need to be objective, not subjective; methodical, not intuitive. Every decision has to be backed up by hard-nosed data, by research, surveys and focus groups. Decisions aren't made on the basis of something as flimsy and unmeasurable as empathy.

That's why we need a big shift in mindset towards a more human approach, one we are not used to using at work. We can't literally *become* our customers, but there are several behaviours that will bring you as close to them as possible.

ACTIONS

UNDERSTAND THE LIMITS OF CUSTOMER DATA

Having access to data is good. But the problem with this less subjective and less risky way of making customer decisions is that hard data, on its own, is just not good enough in this day and age. Your customers' world is changing fast. Their future needs are changing too. Data gives you statistics, it gives you context, but it doesn't give you insight. Data is historical, by definition. It shows you what's already happened. So it's useful to tell you how your old products and services are doing, but it's not going to capture the future or help you design products suited to new, emerging realities. For that you need to understand the human side of the customer experience: What is your product or service really like for the customer? What are their pet peeves? What's missing? What's changing in their world, and what changes to your product would make a major difference to customers? Also, don't forget, your competitors also have access to the same reports, so they're hardly going to give you an edge.

The same is true of customer surveys. Empathy does not mean 'asking customers'. There is no point asking customers, because customers rarely know what they want and so cannot guide you to the future. Before we started Coffee Republic, people told us we should ask customers what they thought of the idea. If we had asked customers if they wanted skinny lattes, or half-caf lattes, most people would have just ticked the box that said they were happy with plain old coffee.

When the Post-It note was invented at 3m, the marketing team, worried about the risky new product, asked customers in a survey if they preferred paper clips or the new innovation that became the Post-It. Customers chose the paperclips. To know what customers really want, you can't ask them. Customers are actually very conservative and often lazy in telling you what they want; I certainly have a lacklustre approach to filling in customer surveys, as I am sure most of us do.

Because entrepreneurs can't afford fancy market research or surveys, they're forced to rely on the simplest, cheapest and most powerful weapon of all – putting themselves in customers' shoes.

SEE EVERYTHING THROUGH CUSTOMERS' EYES

Sure, the statistics and data that BBs have access to are useful – they can help inform your intuition and supplement real-life observations – but they're not enough to spur innovation. Empathy is. If you want to come up with fresh ideas, to see the next opportunity, you have to empathise with customers by experiencing a problem or product as intimately as they do – and in real time.

If you put yourself in customers' shoes whenever possible, their headaches and problems will naturally reveal themselves. Opportunities are just the solutions to these problems, which you can only see them if you are up close and personal with your customers (more on this in the next chapter). When you see and feel for yourself – what in innovation-speak we call *observing* and what anthropologists call *sense-making* – you are generating empathy.

This applies to everyone – not just to the sales or marketing departments. If you have internal customers, then you step into their shoes *and* the shoes of the ultimate customer, so you get a sense of what is needed. Add this level of insight to the data and it's magic.

INNOVATION IS SIMPLY FINDING A SOLUTION TO A CUSTOMER PROBLEM

One of obstacles to innovation is that we put it on a pedestal. In fact, innovation is just finding a solution to a problem. It's not a problem in market share, not a problem your competitors have, it's much more simple than that. It's a problem from your customers' point of view. That's the golden ticket. Finding the next opportunity for your business doesn't start with an executive-mandated hunt for innovation. Nor does it start in a brainstorming session or "innovation day". It starts with something much simpler. It starts with looking for problems to solve.

The problem might be as simple as a tiny mundane process in your organisation, but if it solves what has become a glitch for the customer, it's still innovation. And, simple as it seems, solving problems is the bedrock of being entrepreneurial. As one of America's top start-up investors Paul Graham explains, "*The way to get start-up ideas is not to try to think of start-up ideas. It's to look for problems, preferably problems you have yourself – this ensures the problem really exists. It sounds obvious to say you should only work on problems that exist. And yet by far the most common mistake start-ups make is to solve problems no one has.*" The idea of solving customers' problems applies just as much to big, traditional companies with existing customers as it does to start-ups. Michael Dell says, "*The best customers for us are the ones that present us with a new problem, because chances are, if one customer has that problem, 100 more have it, or 1,000, or 10,000. So you start thinking about solution development rather than product development.*"

Usually at large BBs, if you are told to be 'more innovative' you scramble around doing research and collecting data. You attend a strategy day. You sit through many a brainstorming session. After endless meetings and presentations, a few ideas get the stamp of approval. But when (and if) these ideas are launched, the market often reacts with a shrug. No one really cares; it's innovation for the sake of innovation. It's not solving real problems. That's why leadership guru Peter Diamandis insists "*problems are goldmines*". And the only way to find these problems is to put yourself in customers' shoes and, experience them first hand.

Don't forget the very real (and scary) possibility that there is a customer out there so frustrated by this problem – this *gap* – that you're not seeing that, sooner or later, a start-up will appear bent on solving that problem, and blowing your business out of the water as a result.

AIM FOR CUSTOMER DELIGHT

'Delight' is a word that doesn't fit with traditional management thinking; it's too soft, too unquantifiable, too personal. And yet, it's the basic building block out of which Amazon built a billion-dollar empire. Amazon is one of the most disruptive companies in existence but, unlike many business leaders, founder Jeff Bezos isn't obsessed with disruption. Instead, he claims, *"We don't seek to disrupt, we seek to delight"*. How simple and human is that?

Bezos notes of his competitors, *"When they're in the shower in the morning, they're thinking about how they're going to get ahead of one of their top competitors. Here in the shower, we're thinking about how we are going to invent something on behalf of a customer."* Amazon employees might look like they're shampooing their hair, but mentally they're walking in their customers' shoes, scanning for discomforts to relieve, hassles to eliminate, or opportunities to raise a smile. Other companies wonder, 'How can we innovate?' or 'How can we disrupt?'. Amazon thinks of the customer and works backwards asking, 'How can we help?' or 'How can we delight?'.

Not only is this a more powerful question to ask, it's also simpler to answer.

• • •

Innovation can seem mysterious and difficult, but if you view it instead through the very human capacity for empathy, it becomes much easier. You needn't read the competition's mind or pull ideas out of thin air (or stare at a white board for inspiration). If you put yourself in customers' shoes, all the answers are there, glaringly obvious – all the gaps, all the problems, all the headaches begging to be solved, and therefore all the opportunities. Without empathy you will never see the problems. Empathy makes innovation inevitable. The much sought-after holy grail of "disruptive innovation" is just the by-product of customer empathy. As I said at the beginning of this chapter – start with empathy and everything flows from there.

2

DON'T
SIT AT
YOUR DESK

DO
GET OUT

Empathy only happens when you immerse yourself in the world of your customers

You've seen the power of putting yourself in your customers' shoes and the magic of empathy. But *how* do you get empathy if the nature of your business is such that you are not, and can't become your own customer? If, for example, your company doesn't sell consumer goods, or you work in pharma and obviously can't use with your own products, how can you step into your customer's shoes?

Most of the time the simple solution is getting up from your desk, walking out of the door, and going to see with your own eyes and ears the impact of what you do, whatever it is that you do (even if we're talking about internal customers). This is the only way to cultivate empathy (and innovation), and there's nothing to replace it.

Think of empathy as a kind of spectrum with you on one side, and the your customer on the other.

Maybe you can never be your customer, but you can try to get as close to them as you can.

At Coffee Republic, we pushed our people out into the real world by assigning each new employee a 'pet store' where they would go every morning as a bona fide customer and report on any problems, from queue management to the preparation of their cappuccino, from the customers' point of view. Because they looked with a customer's eyes, they noticed all the detail that a customer would see – and those that a focus group or detached mystery shopper would miss. Each one of those observations was a glitch to solve, aka a new idea.

You might say it was easy for us to do it – we were just sending people out to get a hot chocolate, but trust me, as we became a bigger company with more people, a head office, and more structures, even something as simple as getting people to buy their morning coffee from our own bars became difficult to maintain. People increasingly complained they were just 'too busy' to visit their pet store.

The result was that the details of the experience (through the eyes of a customer) – the perfect music in the background, just the right amount of milk in your Americano, the quality of the pastries

– started to get forgotten amid all the busyness. The only way to notice these details was to be out there in the stores trying and buying the products, and our people no longer had time for that. For me, as a founder, it was painful to watch, because I knew our brand's success was all in the details.

Dan Germaine, who has been at Innocent Drinks since its start-up days, told me he calls it 'lurking and loitering' – referring to the time he spends regularly in the chilled juice aisle of supermarkets. Toyota calls it *genchi gembutsu*, which translates roughly as 'go and see for yourself'. However impossible it might seem at first, there is always a way to see for yourself how your product affects its end users.

ACTIONS

BECOME YOUR OWN MARKET RESEARCH UNIT

We've seen how you can't rely on data and research alone; customers are not statistics, so numbers and figures won't give you the insight you need. Instead, become your own market research unit. If your work involves consumer goods, the way to do this is obvious. Try eating/drinking/

wearing/ using your products and competitors' products in real time, and in the real world. Leave them lingering about at home. Get friends and family to try them. Get your kids to comment on them. That's what entrepreneurs do, and it's amazing how much these very obvious things are simply not done in BBs.

If your product is not as something you can chuck in your bag and bring home at the end of the day, then try instead to get as close as you can to your customers. Be resourceful – this is a creative act. Try to simply observe them, watch them interact with your product, interview them so you get a real understanding of their needs and the challenges they face. Try to feel as much as possible what you would feel, need and want if you were them.

A few years ago, the toy giant Lego stopped listening to core fans of the brand and instead relied on market data, which indicated that children were moving away from bricks and into computer games. New CEO Jurgen Vid Knudstrop sensed disaster ahead and changed direction, encouraging developers and designers to become their own market researchers, sending them to observe families, to see how they shopped, to see the toys they played with. This real-time observation gave Lego a different perspective: old-fashioned play was, in fact, the perfect escape for kids. The blocks came back and the company's fortunes rose.

Getting up close to the customer won't just feed your empathy and generate ideas, it will also power up your creativity on an even more basic level. The fundamental law of creativity is: *quality of stimulus in = quantity of creative ideas out.* A physical change of scene – real-world interaction – often spurs on new thinking, in the same way that travelling does. It's difficult to refresh your thinking when you're sitting at a desk, staring at your computer. PowerPoint presentations and reams of research are not good creative fodder. Nor is brainstorming; brainstorming is useless without the right stimulus. Being outside and observing is where the ideas start, where you can begin to accumulate the creative inputs that will drive innovation. Creative stimulus is a necessary precursor to a successful brainstorming session, not its expected output. Sessions should only be scheduled after everyone has been out there in the real world, refreshing their thinking.

Start-ups understand this, which is why they produce more ideas. Start-ups aren't magically more creative. Entrepreneurs aren't fundamentally more creative people. But without the bubble of an office and a big bureaucracy to shield them, people working in start-ups are much more exposed to creative stimuli. They use their observation muscle, and like any other muscle it grows stronger. Innovation is 'out there', so by being 'out there' – out of a formal office environment, physically occupying the same space, and having the same experiences as their customers – start-ups ensure they're never short of fresh insights.

YOU'RE NEVER TOO IMPORTANT TO BE A MYSTERY SHOPPER

Even a place as mundane as an Ikea checkout line can give you enormous breakthrough insight. Ikea founder Ingvar Kamprad was famous for his commitment to meeting customers on their own turf. One interviewer found him in a most unlikely place, sitting behind a cash register. Why was this a good use of the Ikea tycoon's time, asked the interviewer? *"Because this is the cheapest and the most efficient research ever. I can ask everyone why they choose it and why they didn't choose it,"* replied Kamprad.

Kamprad, a billionaire known for his legendary frugality, insisted on flying in Economy Class – he claimed that would give him an opportunity to observe customers up close much more than in the rarefied luxury of First Class. Howard Schultz of Starbucks, when he returned as CEO, visited twenty-four stores a week. It doesn't matter how busy or senior you are, you're never too important to get out there.

GET AS UP CLOSE AND PERSONAL AS YOU CAN

One of the best ways to get into your customers' minds is to get into their homes. That's the direction that P&G has taken after former CEO A.G. Lafley insisted that managers stop worrying about focus groups and spend time in consumers' homes, watching them cook and clean, before launching new products. In 2000, the typical P&G marketer spent less than four hours a month with consumers; by 2004, that number had tripled.

Employees of Intuit, the makers of accounting software Quicken, call their process 'follow me home'. The company sends employees to watch customers actually boot up the program on their own computers. Why? This is the only way to see how the product works 'in the wild'. Do other programs slow down Quicken? What documents and files are customers looking to access when they use the program? You can't answer those questions unless you are up close to the actual customer experience.

AVOID 'ROYAL VISITS'

You don't need a formal, structured, company-approved and fancy initiative to get results. Phone your own call centre, go online to buy one of your products, serve your food product at dinner or cater a larger gathering, talk to someone who you know is taking medicine made by your pharmaceutical company. These, and countless other forays out into the real world can be incredibly powerful.

Unlike 'royal visits', where everyone knows you are coming, experiencing your products in action and in real time is the only way to make sure you're getting a healthy, well-rounded diet of inspiration. Getting out there takes you into a more creative mindset, it generates the empathy that will drive innovation, observations and conversations in. Insight and ideas out. That's the essential law of innovation.

● ● ●

Creativity is not a unique gift of the lucky few; it's a behavioural shift that you can easily do yourself. So don't wait for a company-approved program to get close to the customer – get out there yourself; do it today; do it now.

3

DON'T BE 'TOO BUSY'

DO ATTACK BUREAUCRACY

Too much bureaucracy distacts you away from your customers' world

If empathy is so easy and common-sense, and going out and seeing for yourself is such a straightforward game-changer, why don't we all do it?

One word – *busyness*.

If you barely have time to wolf down a sandwich at lunchtime, it's not surprising that you don't have time to get out and see customers on their own turf to generate empathy. Finding creative stimulus requires free time. Your calendar, though, is most likely jam-packed from morning to night with meetings, conference calls, reviews, appraisals, strategy days, etc. Even your lunch hour is more of a 'lunch five minutes', a sandwich hastily eaten at your desk between phone calls.

In BBs, the default position is constant busyness. There is a certain comfort in having a full diary. It's 'comfort admin'. Being busy means we are needed and worthy. Busyness means business is good and we are an important part of it. Not being busy feels like alarm bells should be ringing.

The first question to ask in this new world order is: 'Busy doing what, exactly?' Is what we were so 'busy' doing still relevant, when we haven't had time to lift our head and see that the world of our customer is changing on a daily basis? That their habits and choices are not what we thought they were?

Again, start-ups have the advantage here. There is no bureaucracy in a classic three-people-around-a-kitchen-table start-up. If entrepreneurs are busy, it's not in the internal, separate world of a large organisation, but in the same world as that which their customers inhabit. So they are always focused on the external (which is easy enough – there is no internal). They are out there picking up the signals – and much more – in sync with the world of their customer.

I have seen first-hand the contrast between a culture with zero bureaucracy and one where bureaucracy consumes the whole culture. When Coffee Republic grew into a BB, everything changed.

The 'pet store' scheme, for example, that I talked about in the last section, was such a simple premise; how hard could it be to get out there? However, as we became a bigger company with more people, a head office, more structures, more bureaucracy, even something as obvious as getting people to buy their daily coffee from our own stores became difficult to maintain. More and more of our employees' time was spent on internal details like status reports, meetings (and more meetings), and ticking through established procedures. No one had time any more to get out, even though you'd think that getting out would be particularly easy, and attractive, in our industry. People increasingly complained that they were just 'too busy' to visit their pet store. As an entrepreneur I found this frustrating and baffling – what on earth could be more important than seeing the real customer experience up close?

We need to be realistic, of course. You can't run a BB, as Coffee Republic had become, like a five-person start-up – a certain amount of bureaucracy, systems, controls and measures, are essential. It's a question of balance; balance between discipline and creativity. When the balance is out of kilter and unnecessary processes are created, employees spend their time on these processes and customers take a back seat. Or in the harsh but memorable words of Jack Welch, *"A hierarchy is an organisation with its face towards the CEO and its ass to the customer."*

Most people know this; you know this. You know how stultifying bureaucracy can be, but we also usually see it as inevitable. Bureaucracy grows like a weed, and because no one takes the initiative to trim it back, the resulting thicket of rules and procedures becomes the perfect answer to the question, 'Why can't we behave more entrepreneurially? Because we don't have time; we're overloaded as it is!'

So, how do you make time for empathy? Cut your way out of the overgrown tangle of bureaucracy.

ACTIONS

RECLAIM YOUR POWER AND YOUR TIME

What's to be done about this rule creep? Cut it off at its root by taking back control! When asked why they're not more innovative or out observing customers, people often point to an elusive 'they' who won't allow them time for fresh insights. But when pressed, they're usually not able to name exactly who this 'they' is. There isn't a written constitution or magna carta that mandates bureaucracy or weekly conference calls with twenty people on them. The hard but empowering truth is that it's in your power to take control. The processes are not written in stone as unchangeable laws; it's common sense to remove them, one at a time, by looking at your day – from the meetings, to the conference calls, to the weekly check-ins – and culling the ones that aren't absolutely necessary.

MAKE 'BUREAUCRACY-BUSTING' A COMPANY SPORT

Companies that value their entrepreneurial culture tackle bureaucracy head on. Strategies for doing this vary: for example, Google developed 'Bureaucracy Buster', a campaign that encourages people to submit online suggestions for slashing red tape in any shape or form. The most voted for ideas are implemented. The Chinese computer manufacturer, Lenovo, meanwhile, allows its employees to stop staff meetings that have wandered off the agenda.

L'Oréal, in order to keep its challenger status in the beauty industry, specifically focuses on not just pruning back but 'attacking' bureaucracy. Former MD of L'Oréal UK Michel Brousset is a champion of entrepreneurial behaviour. He told me: "*I believe companies are killed not by competition but by the world around them changing. So, the most important thing is to attack bureaucracy to keep everyone facing externally.*"

SCHEDULE EMPTY SLOTS IN YOUR CALENDAR

Another way you can tackle the problem of excessive busyness is to actively schedule free time, a popular strategy among top entrepreneurial leaders.

"I schedule between 90 minutes and two hours of [...] buffers every day (broken down into thirty to 90 minute blocks). It's a system I developed over the last several years in response to a schedule that was becoming so jammed with back-to-back meetings that I had little time left to process what was going on around me or just think," says LinkedIn CEO Jeff Weiner. *"At first, these buffers felt like indulgences... But over time I realised not only were these breaks important, they were absolutely necessary in order for me to do my job,"* he insists.

SMALL IS THE NEW BIG

From my experience with BBs, the perception of the sheer scale of the organisation – the sense it's truly a 'big beast' - is one of the largest obstacles to getting out there and connecting to customers. In a start-up, the people that are making it all happen are both physically and emotionally close. Got something to say? All you need to do is maybe look across the table you share and tell him or her. It's all quite manageable.

The interactions that seem straightforward when you're small become intimidating in a BB. There are chains of commands to consider, boundaries to keep in mind, politics to be mindful of. It's easy to get lost in all that and loose the connection and intimacy with customers.

The solution, once again, is strikingly simple. As best you can, don't think of your organisation as a mass of thousands of people. Instead, divide it up into smaller units, recreating the sensation of personal connection that come naturally in smaller companies.

However large an organisation may be, it is always possible to divide it into small teams. L'Oreal, once again, gets this right. The leadership views the organisation not as a company of 4,000 people, but instead as a company of smaller human-sized units. They have 29 or so brands, so they structure themselves around those brands as 29 small companies.

Online luxury shopping group Net-a-Porter has also ensured that while the company has grown big, it keeps individual teams start-up sized. These small groups can escape BB traffic jams and bring new ideas to life. *"We're organised into about twenty-two teams. Each one of those needs to operate like a start-*

up. What's nice about a start-up is everybody knows what the outcome is, intrinsically. Everybody knows what they're trying to achieve. Nobody can wait a year to see the results. They don't want a big, risky, lengthy, programme of work. Seeing the outcome of their labours in a couple of weeks gets people in the headspace," Hugh Fahy, their former CTO, explains.

Amazon founder Jeff Bezos may have the best, most concise way of capturing this idea of all. He calls it 'the two-pizza rule': a team's size should remain no bigger than that which can be fed by ordering two pizzas, in order to stay agile. Adopt it as your own.

• • •

It's easy to assume that the bureaucracy that locks down your diary and stops you getting outside is an impassable roadblock. You have more power than you think – you *can* find the time to visit, meet and think about your customers. From here, it's just a short step to generating empathy and firing up the creativity that drives innovation and change.

4

DON'T
LET YOUR
KNOWLEDGE
AND EXPERTISE
BLIND YOU

DO
LET GO
OF WHAT
YOU KNOW

There's power in being
a clueless outsider

You can only cultivate a truly open mind if you let go of what you know. A mind full to the brim with knowledge and expertise from years of hard-won experience sounds like an advantage. But in this fast-changing new world it can hold you back. It's highly likely that most of that knowledge and information will soon be obsolete. The experience that was once your most valuable assets starts to work against you, keeping you stuck in the past, unable to see the signals of change that are blasting out at you.

Start-up founders have the advantage of an open mind simply because they are often clueless about the businesses they start. They have no preconceptions, especially not obsolete ones. They often don't have any deep industry knowledge or the ingrained beliefs that come with expertise; they are entering what, for them, is new territory. That gives them a freshness, like the wide-eyed wonder of a tourist visiting a new city for the first time. They see things that would never have been noticed by someone who's lived there for years.

When we came up with the idea for Coffee Republic, we were totally clueless – clueless about coffee, clueless about retail, clueless about catering. We ditched our careers in law and banking to work in an industry about which we knew precisely nothing. I was worried about us being outsiders, about our lack of experience, but I was wrong. In fact, cluelessness proved to be our biggest advantage. Our naivety gave us a fresh outlook on the traditional coffee bars that had been around for centuries. All we saw in our blissful cluelessness was our vision, which was simple – to open in the UK one of those coffee bars with which I had fallen in love in New York.

If cluelessness is the secret sauce of entrepreneurship, the opposite is generally true of BBs. Their success and expertise – which got them where they are – eventually becomes their Achilles' heel. It's human nature. Research shows that our brains make us prone to repeat what we have done in the past, especially if it was successful. We switch on the autopilot. The result is that, instead of being tourists wondering in awe at a foreign city, we become like the commuter who travels the same route day after day, ignoring our surroundings, never looking up to notice new landmarks or the change of seasons.

Success is great but it's also a trap. Knowledge and experience weigh you down. That's why Steve Jobs celebrated getting fired from Apple in his famous commencement speech. *"The heaviness of being successful was replaced by the lightness of being a beginner again, less sure about everything. It freed me to enter one of the most creative periods of my life,"* he told Stanford grads.

I saw that "heaviness of being successful" creep in in at Coffee Republic. While a lot of our initial team were as clueless as we were, once we started attracting people with good CVs and experience in the coffee industry, it became clear that our 'dream hires' also brought with them all the baggage that accompanies experience.

All of a sudden, new changes were met with disapproval and warnings, as the voices of experience resisted any attempt to try new things, giving endless reasons why every little change wouldn't work. Instead of the blissful naivety of our early days, there was a status quo, a tried and trusted way of doing things. It became so easy to dismiss untested new ideas. When you hold gravitas up against the insubstantiality of an unproven idea, we know which one has the most credibility. New ideas are just so easy to undermine, to discount.

"Don't watch the giant in front of you. Watch the maverick behind you" is a quote that really resonates with me. Companies are obsessed with their competitors, but very often, BBs are overtaken not by their fellow giants, or by some outsider maverick with no pre-suppositions or expertise. As innovation guru, Clayton Christensen says, "When a large organization falls, it's not generally another expert that took it down." Of course, expertise can be a great asset, but when the pace of change is so swift, expertise can very quickly become obsolete. As top investor Paul Graham says, "When experts are wrong, it's often because they're experts on an earlier version of the world."

So how can BBs capitalise on the upside of expertise and experience but avoid it becoming an anchor tethering them to the past? How can they look at their business with fresh eyes – like the tourist, not the commuter? In short, how does someone with valuable experience and expertise become clueless again?

ACTIONS

POLICE THE LANGUAGE YOU USE

Language is a powerful tool for shaping both individual thought and company culture. How often do you hear these phrases being bandied about at your workplace?

- *This is how we do things.*
- *It's industry practice.*
- *We tried that already.*
- *Believe me, this won't work.*
- *Yes, but...*

These phrases are an accepted part of the office lexicon, and yet they are so destructive. They assume that past experience and superior knowledge give us the best perspective on the viability of a new idea. These phrases shut off our creativity by scolding us for looking with wide-eyed awe, implying instead that we should put our heads back down and stop exploring. Instead of asking the open-minded question – like, simply, 'Why?' -- the sentiment communicated becomes 'Why bother?' And that pushes us into automaton mode. There's something condescending about this language, which breeds complacency and fear of change.

Consider replacing these phrases (in your own vocabulary, or that of your team) with more open-minded responses so you can break away from the past and look at new ideas with clear eyes. Try these alternatives:

- This is how we do things. *Let's try this way.*
- It's industry practice. *It's interesting.*
- We tried that already. *Let's give it a try.*
- Believe me, this won't work. *Let's see what happens.*
- Yes, but… *Yes, and…*

It pays to become aware of your language, so that it stops being normal to denigrate new ideas. This is a subtle shift, but these tiny changes really do influence culture enormously. Perhaps consider a swear jar for these axioms: every time someone lets one slip out they have to contribute to the next office lunch or outing.

Or follow the example of the colourful founders of Method, the highly innovative non-toxic cleaning product company (that was recently bought by SC Johnson). They were the people who first introduced me to a theatre improv practice that they regularly use: when someone shares a new idea the words 'Yes but…' are banned. Instead, everyone must respond with 'Yes and…'. This stops people immediately discounting new ideas, and forces them instead to explore and build on them.

HIRE FOR WILL, NOT SKILL

Think about hiring for enthusiasm, empathy and curiosity rather than just experience – for will, rather than for skill. Start-ups rarely attract those with golden CVs and decades' worth of accumulated experience, so they learn to focus on will, attitude, and enthusiasm. From my experience, this works out well. When we could afford to hire great CVs and industry veterans at Coffee Republic, that's when our culture started changing. On the other hand, it's easier to teach skills than most people imagine, but it's impossible to teach enthusiasm.

"*We would rather take an eager, hungry, customer-oriented mind and mould it to what works well at Southwest, than try to change the habits of someone who's come up through an organisation that views life differently,*" says Sherry Phelps, a veteran HR executive at hugely innovative Southwest Airlines. This same thinking is why so many companies refuse to hire people from the same industry. Max Conze, CEO of Dyson, agrees: "*Our process for hiring is a bit unconventional, like a lot of things at Dyson. Rather than looking for specific experience, we tend to hire young, fresh graduates. They come in with big ideas, unsullied by the weight of experience, which can often temper these grand thoughts.*"

BREAK THROUGH SILOS BY MIXING UP YOUR TEAMS

Getting fresh perspectives is not just about bringing in fresh perspectives from outside the company. Breaking down internal silos so that teams can mix and ask those in different areas of the business to contribute new ideas encourages open-minded thinking too. Getting marketing to sit in on a HR meeting, or vice versa, allows non-experts to voice the sort of fundamental but powerful questions that the experts often fail to ask.

• • •

By changing language and taking expertise off the pedestal, you remove the barriers to the sort of open, receptive mind that is needed to respond to fast-changing customer needs. Innovation is essentially an act of creative destruction – we cannot find new ways when we're stuck in the old ones. We can't see new possibilities when we are holding on to obsolete beliefs. Unlearning is key.

As Paul Graham says, *"The best strategy is simply to be aggressively open-minded. Instead of trying to point yourself in the right direction, admit you have no idea what the right direction is, and try instead to be super sensitive to the winds of change."*

Open-mindedness is everything. Admitting you don't know the 'right way' is critical. A clueless mind removes the shame of asking the naïve questions and replaces it with an invigorating curiosity (more on that in the next section).

5

DON'T
SUFFOCATE
CURIOSITY

DO
BE A
BIG KID

Asking stupid questions
is a clever thing to do

I ended the last section with a quote from Paul Graham about being aggressively open-minded. Instead of trying to find the right direction, he recommends, *"Admitting we have no idea what the right direction is and being super sensitive to the winds of change."* We know how important it is to be clueless, to cultivate an open mind. Clueless people see things that others don't; they have a wide-eyed wonder that allows their imagination to expand in a way that those of people weighed down with expertise just can't. And breaking with the past is essential for creating an open mind.

There is one further element, though, without which an open mind is meaningless – curiosity. *"Surely it's easy to be curious,"* you say. *"It's human nature. It's nothing new."* But being truly curious is an art – and curiosity deserves a chapter all to itself. Commonsense traits are never as intuitive as you might believe, especially when you try to put them into practice – and especially not in BBs.

In a 2018 survey of 3,000 employees conducted by Harvard Business School Professor Francesca Gino, only 24% reported feeling curious in their jobs on a regular basis, and 70% felt they faced barriers to asking more questions at work. That's because there is a bravado that comes with corporate culture that stifles curiosity. It's a bravado which means that, as leader (or aspiring leader), you are 'the adult in the room', a figure of authority. You are meant to know everything, to have all the answers and to be in total control. So, any question that implies ignorance inevitably makes leaders worry they might appear weak or inadequate, when leaders should be a source of strength and solutions.

At a start-up, however, there is no bravado. You cannot *not* ask questions – it's a matter of necessity. You wear your outsider status on your sleeve, like a badge of honour. No one expects you to be 'the adult in the room'. You are the curious, questioning maverick – there's no pressure on you to be anything else.

When we were starting Coffee Republic it was all about the questions we kept asking. The questions *were* the ideas: *How do we convert a nation of tea drinkers to latte drinkers? How do you make a Frappuccino like Starbucks?*

What can we serve children when they come in with their parents? How can we stop people walking out of long queues? The list went on and on. Our questions were limitless and, therefore, so were our ideas.

Recent research says that children ask around a staggering seventy-three questions a day. This number naturally decreases as we age and learn more answers. But as a management tool, child-like questions can be incredibly powerful. Take the example of Edwin Land. He was a chemist, inventor and amateur photographer, but his most famous idea didn't spring from any of these areas of expertise. Instead, it came from his three-year-old daughter who just wouldn't stop asking why she couldn't see a picture as soon as it was taken. The result of her nagging – the Polaroid camera – went on to sell more than 150 million units and wrote Land (co-founder of the Polaroid company) into the history books.

It is human nature to feel that every time we put our hands up, we take a risk. We fear we might be seen as stupid. But through my years of entrepreneurship, I have learnt that if we were to think hard about every question we ask, weighing up the pros and cons, we would never ask one and would instead keep our hands forever down. Entrepreneurship honed my questioning muscles – my curiosity. I'm never shy of asking even the most obvious questions, no matter whom I'm talking to. Through practice, I have found that the power actually lies in the asking.

How can people in BBs encourage curiosity? How can you remove the stigma and fear of asking questions and appearing like you might not have all the answers?

ACTIONS

MAKE IT MORE THAN OK TO SHOW VULNERABILITY

The bravado that comes with the old corporate culture – that mask of knowing all the answers – needs to shift as companies enter a new era. Bravado might have been a strength once, but now it's a weakness. It closes your mind. It's actually fear in disguise – fear of being judged, fear of looking stupid, and (most detrimentally) fear of the new. This bravado, a residue of the old cultural template, needs to be replaced by its opposite, vulnerability. By encouraging vulnerability in the workplace, you remove the mask of bravado, making it OK not to know, OK to ask stupid questions, OK not to be 100% certain of every outcome. Innovation cannot happen without vulnerability.

Vulnerability's most famous champion is University of Houston research professor Brené Brown. Her TED talk on the Power of Vulnerability is among the top five most-viewed of all time. Brown argues that vulnerability is not about being weak or submissive. Showing our vulnerability is actually the most courageous thing we can do. It liberates us to be our most authentic and effective selves.

For curiosity to flourish in a BB you have to remove the bravado. Leaders need to encourage vulnerability as a strength, removing its stigma. As Bill George, ex-CEO of Medtronics and now Harvard Business School professor, whose leadership course remains one of my most memorable experiences, says, *"Vulnerability is freedom".* Once you learn to embrace that, and remove the bravado, you see the real power in asking the questions.

BE THE 'CHIEF STUPID QUESTION-ASKER'

It's about setting the tone by example. Leaders can encourage curiosity by becoming 'chief question askers'. If those at the top show curiosity by questioning the status quo, bravely admitting 'I don't know', and asking the seemingly naïve questions, others will be encouraged to do the same.

Hollywood producer Brian Grazer calls this 'leading by curiosity'. *"If you're the boss, and you manage by asking questions, you're laying the foundation for the culture of your company or your group".*

REPLACE 'HOW SHOULD WE...?' WITH 'HOW MIGHT WE?'

Another approach is to simply to change your vocabulary. The HMW approach is as straightforward as it is possible to be. While working at Proctor & Gamble, Min Basadur discovered that just swapping the judgmental-sounding 'How can we...?' or 'How should we...?' for the more positive, open-ended, and curious 'How might we...?' HMW removed the weight and seriousness from discussions, allowing his team to become more playful and, therefore, braver.

Facebook, Google and world-leading design firm IDEO now all use the HMW technique. *"The 'How' part assumes there are solutions out there — it provides creative confidence. 'Might' says we can put ideas out there that might work or might not — either way, it's OK. And the 'We' part says we're going to do it together and build on each other's ideas,"* says IDEO CEO Tim Brown, explaining why the method is so effective.

• • •

Effective but simple tools to encourage curiosity do exist. And they're not just useful in your work life. They can transform your personal outlook too (the two are intimately tied together, after all). As I get older, I'm conscious of jadedness creeping in. My mind is becoming contaminated with memories of the past — good and bad — and, along with them, preconceptions about how things should or inevitably will be done. It's surprisingly easy to lose the naivety, and the hunger. But then I look around and am inspired by people — not the ones who 'know a lot' but those who, at whatever age, remain childlike and curious.

Henry Ford summed it up perfectly. I have his words framed and hanging over my desk: *"Anyone who stops learning is old, whether at twenty or eighty. Anyone who keeps learning stays young."*

Curiosity, in other words, won't just make you more creative and successful at work; it will also keep you young. And all it takes is a few simple shifts in how you approach and talk about the world.

6

DON'T BUY INTO THE FAIRYTALE ROMANCE OF THE 'BIG IDEA'

DO ACT ON THE SMALL EVERYDAY IDEAS

The only way to know if an idea is good is by acting on it

As I wrote in my first book, *Anyone Can Do It*, if you have an idea, you are only 0.01% down the road of entrepreneurship. 'An idea not acted upon is worthless' is a central truth of entrepreneurship. You may have heard that oft-repeated Thomas Edison quote conveying the same message: *"Genius is one percent inspiration and ninety-nine percent perspiration."*

When it comes to creating an innovation-friendly culture, the first thing anyone working in a BB needs to do is to liberate themselves from the myth of the 'Big Idea'. Take ideas off the pedestal. Scott Burkan, in his book *The Myths of Innovation*, talks about the myth of epiphany – 'the sudden manifestation' of an idea. The biggest of them all is the story of Isaac Newton and the discovery of gravity. According to Burkan, the popular legend – that Newton was sitting under a tree when an apple fell on his head, and thus the idea of gravity was born – discounts twenty years of work and iteration which in fact produced the discovery of gravity. It's a good tale, but it doesn't tell anything like the whole story.

Burkan goes on to say that most of the major innovations of our time happened without epiphanies. The World Wide Web wasn't born out of a eureka moment but came instead out of years and years of discovery, experimentation and iteration. As Amazon founder Jeff Bezos put it, "*There wasn't a sense of, my God, we've invented this incredible thing that nobody has seen before and it will just take over.*" As Burkan puts it, Bezos and others, "*instead recognised a set of opportunities and set about capitalizing on them.*"

For entrepreneurs, ideas – like the starting whistle in a race – are just the beginning of the process. This was true of my own entrepreneurial experience. The initial idea, the 'lightbulb' moment that we had, to bring US-style coffee bars to the UK, was neither unique, nor valuable. We were among a cast of thousands. So many people have told me that they, too, fell in love with the US-style coffee bars. They, too, had 'the idea'. But we became entrepreneurs because we actually ran with the idea. That first spark of an idea – chatting at a Thai restaurant – drove me to spend a whole day on the Circle Line doing market research. Then I wrote the business plan. Then went to meet potential suppliers. With one action, then another, and another, the idea that had been just between our ears grew and gained momentum.

Ideas by themselves are as significant and as sturdy as a puff of air. They require action to grow into something useful and tangible. No idea arrives fully formed and ready to slap on a PowerPoint slide and present to the world. Getting there is always a process of development and discovery.

That's a truth BBs often misunderstand, and that misapprehension kills an incredible number of good ideas. Often, I find, everyone in the organisations I work with is waiting for the proverbial 'Big Idea' – the game-changing insight that arrives whole and complete out of the clear blue sky. They endlessly wait for epiphanies. Because of this, they discount or ignore the thousands of small, half-baked, imperfect opportunities for change – the problems to be solved – that crop up day in and day out in their organisations and that can add up to big thinking. To large organisations that's not innovation, just small, unimportant annoyances. 'Come back when you've got all the details nailed down and then we'll act on it,' they say.

The result can be one of two things. Either these companies do nothing to act on their people's everyday creativity, as these half-baked ideas and tiny sparks of possible innovation aren't (at least at first) the million-dollar idea they are expecting. So, without action, these ideas evaporate. Or, they put too much rigorous scrutiny on newborn ideas, trying to project future earnings, debating their merits endlessly, and opening every idea up to criticism by dozens. The fragile idea, untested in the world, flickers and dies out.

The result is that people learn that ideas don't make a difference and are not worth mentioning, so no one bothers to come up with any (or if they have them, they certainly don't mention them). The self-fulfilling prophecy that new ideas will promptly be killed gets embedded into the culture. How do you undo this damage and convince people to believe in ideas again? How can BBs become breeding and testing grounds for new ideas? How can they nurture these sparks rather than kill them??

ACTIONS

GET A 'DEAL FLOW' OF IDEAS

The first step is to stop romanticising ideas. To begin thinking creatively, like an entrepreneur, all you need to do is stop looking for the big idea, the game changer. Fully formed ideas will not fall on your head like Newton's apple. Ideas are much less glamorous. They start out small. An idea might be just a solution to a problem you've seen when you're immersed in the world of your customer, or a set of incremental changes you can make to mundane processes.

The second step is to stop thinking you can predict whether or not an idea will work. You can't show future earnings on the basis of an idea alone, nor will endless debates accompanied by PowerPoint slides reveal which ideas will actually work. Instead of trying to analyse ideas, act on them. Instead of discussing, experiment. Even if these efforts are quick, dirty, small-scale, imperfect. In fact, this sort of cheap and fast testing of ideas is preferable, as that way you can afford to test more of them.

Cheap and fast is good because you need a 'deal flow' of ideas. *"Want to have a good idea?"* asks David Blakely of IDEO, *"Have a lot of ideas."* There is no way to identify the mythical 'one big idea' in its infancy. Instead, if you want to eventually come up with one massive, game-changing idea, act on and test as many small ideas as possible. If you make ideas sacred – and therefore expensive and rare – you all but guarantee you'll never come up with a good one. Make them cheap and plentiful and you increase your chances exponentially.

TURN IDEAS INTO "LET ME SHOW YOU WHAT I MEAN" PROTOTYPES ASAP

As soon as you get an idea, start acting on it. Don't wait till it's fully baked. The important thing is to turn that creative possibility into something tangible as quickly as possible, and then start refining it by iteration.

Start-ups do this all the time. There is a lot of jargon used to capture this behaviour – you might hear about 'minimum viable product' or 'lean methodology' or, in the design world, 'prototyping', but the basic idea is incredibly simple. Start building something small, based on your idea, and then tinker with it. In everyday language, entrepreneurs experiment. They turn ideas from something abstract into something you can see, touch, or feel so they can evolve into something great.

James Dyson didn't just have an epiphany prior to producing the world's first bagless vacuum cleaner. It wasn't an '*a-ha!*' moment. He famously made

5,217 prototypes of his namesake product with loo rolls and tape before hitting on a successful design of the Dyson as we now know it. The process took him eighteen-odd years.

For me, personally, as soon as I get an idea, I start a to-do list. I still have the ones I did for both my businesses. It starts with the mundane – find prices, find suppliers, find a site – but all those mundane steps move us from an abstract idea to actionable tasks we can complete each day. I still do exactly this for every venture I undertake, including my books.

Acting on your ideas in this way is important. First, because it aids communication. When you start turning an idea into something physical, you're able to say, "Let me show you what I mean." That helps people 'get it' much better than trying to capture an idea in words. A concept or product that might sound crazy in the abstract can suddenly reveal its genius when someone can physically see what you're talking about.

More importantly, giving an idea physical shape and testing it out with real, live people provides incredibly valuable feedback which helps to refine the idea. Actions bring momentum. But BBs have this backward. They wait for an idea to be perfect before they act on it. This unconscious quest for perfection stops ideas being tested and developed. Ironically, it's waiting around for perfect ideas that prevents organisations from ever having any good ones. Without momentum, ideas die.

Acting on unproven, half-baked ideas is perhaps the most powerful thing that entrepreneurs do when it comes to innovation. The only obstacle to your organisation taking the same approach is the endless quest for the beautiful, fully-formed 'big idea'. Throw away every imperfect idea and none are left.

PUT A 'FRAGILE: HANDLE WITH CARE!' SIGN ON NEW IDEAS

Many BBs don't realise how fragile ideas are before they're made into something tangible. Subjecting a half-baked, untested idea to the scrutiny of a large group of uncommitted people who have every incentive to be critical of it is akin to wearing a meat suit in a cage of tigers. In *Anyone Can Do It* I refer to the famous quote (origins disputed): *"An idea is delicate. It can be killed by a sneer or a yawn; it can be stabbed to death by a joke or worried to death by a frown on the right person's brow."*

Ed Catmull, head of hugely innovative animation studio Pixar, has a memorable expression that captures this truth about newborn ideas well. Far from being shining, beautiful, and instantly compelling, Catmull calls new ideas 'ugly babies'.

"A new thing is hard to define; it's not attractive, and it requires protection," he has written. *"Pixar is set up to protect our director's ugly baby."*

How do you protect your 'ugly babies' and allow them to grow into beautiful fully-fledged adult ideas? You do what entrepreneurs do: you act on them rather than put them out there for scrutiny and criticism by committee. That way, by the time people within your organisation see them, they are not so half-baked anymore. Instead, they are tangible, modified and adjusted based on the feedback received from your small trusted team who put themselves in customers' shoes. They have momentum behind them. That makes them far less vulnerable.

● ● ●

The bottom line is this: when you have an idea, however small, insignificant, half baked or uncertain it is, you need to just start. Don't wait for the 'biggie'. See past the romance of the idea that might 'revolutionise' your business. Don't procrastinate and, for sure, don't over-plan – or even plan at all. Instead, be willing to take the long and crooked path that runs through lots of half-formed, mistake-filled experiments. Think of those in the same way as the 5,127 imperfect ideas that James Dyson acted on – the 5,128th one will be right. Here in the real world that is the only way that innovation happens.

7

DON'T
LET PERFECTIONISM
SLOW YOU DOWN

DO
FORCE THE
DISCIPLINE
OF
BOOTSTRAPPING

Bootstrapping overrides the complexity and slowness that kills ideas

Once you've nurtured your ideas (your ugly babies), developing them into something more tangible, it's time for them to leave the protection of the company nest. They need to launch as quickly as possibly into the world to meet, interact with and be tweaked by contact with actual customers. But it's at this critical execution stage, that ideas often get stuck in a BB.

Why is that? The two most common excuses I hear time and time again from BBs as to why ideas never make it out into the real world is either lack of resources or that ideas get stuck in a corporate traffic jam. They fall into the cracks between departments or get held up waiting for multiple authorisations. They lose momentum somehow. This is especially true in times of change. In hard times, you need to innovate your way out of trouble, yet, paradoxically, this is when budgets are most squeezed, and leadership can be most cautious about green lighting new projects.

But if resources are so important for innovation, then how is it that start-ups, who don't have one-hundredth the resources, manpower, contacts, or systems, are so far ahead of BBs? It's because start-ups are adept at bootstrapping. They have learnt to do whatever it takes to make things happen. The image of a lone entrepreneur using minimal resources and maximum initiative to launch (the definition of bootstrapping) is an essential part of start-up culture.

The importance of bootstrapping for the start-up ethos isn't just an accident of circumstance – it's not just because all those founders, whose stories we have read about, happened to start out in a garage or kitchen with next to nothing. Resources have an adverse effect on innovation. They create a lazy mindset. Counter-intuitively, resources can restrict you. And, in fact, lack of resources has the opposite effect, making you more innovative. As IDEO founder Tom Kelley says in his book *Creative Confidence*, *"One way to spark creative action is to constrain it – constraints can spur creativity and incite action as long as you have the confidence to embrace them."*

Bootstrapping isn't just an approach to financial constraints; it's a mindset of extreme resourcefulness, a way of doing things "by hook or by crook". If you learn to bootstrap, you can get things done, whether resources are scarce or abundant. You learn to disregard silos, not letting them get in the way. It gives you the confidence Tom Kelley talks about in the quote above, the confidence to embrace the constraints that spark creative action.

We have seen in earlier sections how circumstances – for example, a lack of bureaucracy or experience – make start-ups behave in certain ways. Another of those circumstances is what might, at first, look like a big weakness: lack of resources. Cash-strapped entrepreneurs are forced, out of necessity, to squeeze every last drop from what they have to get their business off the ground. So bootstrapping becomes their biggest strength as it teaches them to do things fast, to make things happen, to build momentum. And once you have momentum on your side, the rest is history.

When we were building Coffee Republic, we had nothing at our disposal – a very limited budget, and no network of suppliers or resources we could access. Coffee bars as we had seen them in New York didn't exist, so the supply network to provide the equipment we needed didn't exist either. That meant we had to bootstrap by stealing our first employees from Pret A Manger, importing cups very expensively from the US and putting stickers on them ourselves, and baking those special muffins at home. Somehow, we had to make 2+2=5. We made it work with whatever we had to hand. It was totally imperfect, but it got the business off the ground.

We usually think of bootstrapping as a way to economise and reduce expenditure, but the truth is, the discipline it requires doesn't just save time and money, it also spurs creativity. Or, as The Body Shop founder, the late Dame Anita Roddick, memorably put it: *"If I'd had shed loads of money, I'd have done everything wrong."*

Actually, when we became big and successful and people were throwing money at us, we got less creative because we didn't need to bootstrap anymore. In the early days, if we wanted new branding, my brother and I spent hours with our lone graphic designer in his attic office focusing on every little detail of our brand, really honing the messages we wanted to give to customers. Later when we became a BB, our marketing manager would contact the big graphic design agency, and mood boards and ideas would be produced by a team of seven (many of whom had probably never even been to one of our stores). It all became so corporate and sterile. So detached. We lost that close, connected feeling to the little details of our brand and therefore to the heart of our business.

That's why bootstrapping is such an important

behaviour shift for BBs. It might appear constraining and stressful, but it's actually the opposite –imposing conscious constraints can be immensely liberating. Bootstrapping makes things happen and gives momentum. Without it, innovation gets stuck in internal BB traffic jams. How exactly do you bootstrap in a BB when it's not out of necessity?

ACTIONS

CONSTRAIN YOUR RESOURCES TO FIND OUT HOW RESOURCEFUL YOU ARE

Even if you don't have to scrimp like an entrepreneur, it can pay to think like one. If institutional support, systems, and processes tend to kill innovation, then your first step should be to rely less on company resources, even if your organisation can afford to give them to you. Instead, work with a limited budget and under the radar of established systems. If you impose (artificial) constraints – for example, acting small with a small team, small budget, and limited time frame – then you and your team will be 'forced' to be creative and to suck every ounce out of the resources you have to hand in any way you can. It will be a new way of thinking and acting that is much more likely to get your ideas off the ground.

Google consciously forces the discipline imposed by a lack of resources on its people, knowing that – even though the company can certainly afford more – employees will accomplish so much more with less. At a lunch I attended with Lars Rasmussen, founder of Google Maps, he talked about one of Google's biggest failures, Google Wave. The biggest mistake they made, he said, was to put all the might of Google behind this project. He added that it was a big lesson for Google, which has subsequently adopted the 'scarcity leads to clarity' motto. As Google co-founder Sergey Brin has written, *"[Scarcity] focuses minds, forcing people to think creatively and rise to the challenge."*

ANYTHING WORTH DOING IS WORTH DOING BADLY

Like most other entrepreneurs, my motto is, *"Anything worth doing is worth doing badly."* The saying is so popular because starting a new business shows you the unconscious quest for perfection runs counter to entrepreneurial behaviour. It slows things down. That's true for newborn ideas when they are first being developed within the organisation, and it's true when the time comes to test those ideas in the market. It's all about speed: being quick, so you can get your idea out there, adapt, tweak and iterate.

When the founders of Airbnb had their billion-dollar idea, for example, they didn't pay thousands on thousands for a top designer to build them a beautiful website. Instead, they immediately set up a simple page. The initial 'product' was just a few pictures of the founders' empty apartment, but the most important thing was they made something and put it out in the world. Online shoe retailer Zappos's first website was simply photos of shoes taken by co-founder Nick Swinmurn. When someone ordered a pair, Swinmurn went to a store, bought them, and mailed them. It was low-tech in the extreme, and very cost-ineffective, but it proved that the market was there for an online shoe store. The rest is history.

But the first Zappos or Airbnb products would never have been approved in a BB. They were too imperfect, too unbaked. The idea would have been stuck in the corporate traffic jam and never seen the light of day. In his book, *Start-up of You*, LinkedIn founder Reid Hoffman says that, for entrepreneurs, the real F-word is 'finished'. Products should always be in test phase, so that their makers can tinker with and improve them as customers respond to them. He calls the mindset 'permanent beta'. Gmail, for instance, was launched in 2004 but was left in beta until 2009, by which point millions were already using it.

In just the same way, new restaurants don't suddenly open to the public, they often hold 'soft openings', where they test out their food and concept on a limited number of customers for a few days or weeks, improving as they go.

BOOTSTRAPPING CIRCUMVENTS SILOS

We all know the importance of execution, and that innovation is really about executing ideas, not having them. And that's where the silo mentality in BBs halts innovation. In order to happen, an innovation has to pass through different departments – production, marketing, sales – with little communication and closeness between each one. So inevitably, things get stuck.

When I sold my sugar-free candy business, Skinny Candy, to a big confectionary conglomerate, for example, I was so pleased that they had a huge sales team. I had done the selling myself and had gotten it into major supermarkets, so it was a huge relief to learn that this team had experience, and contacts with major players like Tesco. I thought they could sell it easily; but I was wrong. In fact, they were so used to selling the well-known, established brands that they didn't have the passion or understanding to sell a maverick sugar-free product. They didn't believe in it enough and didn't have the resilience to push through the rejections this new, unknown product was getting. So, of course, they couldn't sell it at all. It was even delisted at the major supermarkets where I had already sold it. That's when I learnt how important it is to follow a new idea right through to the end and not leave the implementation bit to someone without a close connection.

In start-ups, the same person takes an idea through to the finish line. In the words of Paul Graham, *"The needs of the customer and the means of satisfying them are all in one head."* There aren't any departments, and the founders have to wear each of those many different hats themselves. As I said in *Anyone Can Do It*, as an entrepreneur you have to be *'chief cook and bottle-washer'* at the same time. So, in effect, start-ups are forced to be cross-functional, which leads to consistency and follow-through. That's why BBs need to break silos and create small, cross-functional teams to make an innovation happen. The same team needs to see an idea through from start to finish.

Of course, in BBs there will never be lone mavericks taking products single-handedly from idea status to the customer's front door. But that doesn't mean that these businesses don't need to maintain the connection between an idea's originator – the person or group with the greatest passion for, and understanding of, the product – and its execution all the way through the development process.

• • •

In a BB it is so important that ideas don't get stuck at the planning stage, or blocked, or shut down prematurely, and the only way to really prevent this happening is to impose constraints – even if they are artificial ones. That's why bootstrapping is such an important discipline to consciously instill in a BB. Imposing limitations on budgets and resources encourages bootstrapping and that, in turn, encourages resourcefulness. Bootstrapping takes people away from the perfectionist mindset, from the fear of doing anything until they are sure it will be perfect. It is fun, creative and quick... In a world where size is a liability because it slows you down, bootstrapping overrides complexity and gives you speed.

8

DON'T
BE SCARED
OF FAILURE

DO
ENCOURAGE
IT

Celebrating failure turns off fear and turns up creativity

Failure is something that just isn't tolerated in adulthood. Stumbling is fine for toddlers. When they fall down, it's the cue for everyone to clap with joy, because it is just part of the learning process. This trial-and-error learning process is fine for the young, but once we reach adulthood, it's different. Everyone expects that, by the time you reach maturity, you've learnt those lessons, you've made the stumbles, and now it's time for stability, for success – not mistakes and failure.

This 'young and old' analogy applies to the growth of businesses too. It is fine to fail if you're a small start-up. But once you 'grow up' into a BB, failure is not tolerated. The corporate model of command and control has been specifically built to avoid risk and failure. Good performance means avoiding failure. Careers, reputations and pay are all at stake if a mistake is made. The price of failure is huge. And so, of course, the fear of failure in these companies is correspondingly huge, almost crippling.

This fear of failure is perhaps the biggest obstacle to entrepreneurial behavior and has the potential to undermine every shift in this book — as every one is based on acting and doing, fear can cripple each one. Fear inhibits action. Fear stops you getting out of the office to get close to your customers, it stops you asking the naïve questions, and it stops you acting on your ideas, testing them and experimenting. And, most importantly, it's not a very pleasant place to be.

The popular vision of entrepreneurs as swashbuckling risk takers who don't fear failure is a fallacy. Entrepreneurs aren't gamblers. They're not adrenaline junkies. There's no magic chromosome or personality trait that takes away their fear of failure. They fear failure like everyone else does — but they don't let this fear stop them. The difference lies, firstly, in their attitude to failure; and secondly, their need for momentum. Entrepreneurs think differently about failure. They know the only way to avoid making a mistake, or failing, is to do nothing — and for them, doing nothing is not an option. They know that doing *something* - gaining momentum - is so critical.

The key is not to let the fear get the better of you. My brother and I left safe, successful careers to open a chain of coffee shops – something about which we knew next to *nothing*. As we embarked on the journey together, we realised immediately that sitting for days weighing up the pros and cons, worrying what we'd do if the venture collapsed, asking around for random advice, just looking at the edge of the cliff we were about to jump off, wasn't going to work. Instead, we just jumped, putting aside our fears and doubts, pressing the DELETE button on them, and getting started. Since then, my own attitude to failure has always been, 'Leap, and the net will appear.'

People still ask me how I dealt with the fear. *"Weren't you worried? How did you know coffee bars would work in this country?"*

The truth is we never dealt with the fear. We were in the flow, too busy acting on the idea we had. We never had time to sit staring at the abyss and asking ourselves: did we make the right decision? Should we continue or give up? Thank God we didn't – if we had, we wouldn't have persevered. Instead, we focused on working through our to-do list, day by day, obstacle by obstacle, one little goal at a time.

In a BB, doing nothing is an easy and wholly viable option (in the short-term, at least). You can get on with business as usual – swamped by bureaucracy (see section 2), tucked right back in your comfort zone and letting unconscious fear get the better of you.

So, how do you prevent fear stopping you?

ACTIONS

MAKE LITTLE BETS

People mistake the risk-taking of entrepreneurial behavior, or trying out new ideas, with gambling. It's a huge misnomer. We've already seen the value of acting on many ideas, of small experiments and bootstrapping. Doing things on a small scale, with limited resources, reduces the cost of failure and so, correspondingly, takes away the fear of failure because you're not betting the house. If projects are large-scale and company-wide, the sums are much greater, and the price of failure is enormous. Peter Sims lays out the connection between small, clever risks and creativity in his book *Little Bets*. By placing many small bets, he explains, companies can limit the downside of failure while still benefiting from its huge upsides. Make a project, initiative or experiment small, and the fear of getting it wrong becomes proportionately small.

GIVE PEOPLE PERMISSION TO FAIL

The first step is to explicitly give permission to fail by removing the stigma of failure. Many people within BBs retain vivid memories of being punished for failures, however subtle that punishment may have been. They've internalized the stigma of failure. If you are a leader, you need, through your words and actions, to promote a culture that takes away fear of failure by removing that stigma. Doing so can be as straightforward as a label change: leaders might stop talking about 'failures' and start talking about 'experiments' and 'important learning opportunities.'

Michel Brousset at L'Oréal understands this. "*One of the biggest obstacles to entrepreneurship is fear so you have to create a culture where fear of failure is not part of it,*" he explained to me. "*Mistakes happen, failure happens, instead of punishing or throwing in the towel, what can we learn from it?*"

There are plenty of different ways to learn from

failure. P&G encourages employees to talk about their failures as well as their successes during performance reviews. Indian conglomerate Tata offers a prize for the Best Failed Idea, which publicly rewards smart but unsuccessful projects. Food company Innocent also gathers employees regularly to discuss mistakes without shame, so the whole company can learn from them. Software company Intuit and pharmaceutical giant Eli Lilly have both taken to holding 'failure parties' where participants openly discuss their screw ups. When people do start taking more risks and (as is sometimes inevitable) fail, their efforts need to be met with praise, not a demotion. Google knows this. The team behind the famously doomed Google Wave product weren't dismissed; they were celebrated. *"They took a massive, calculated risk. And failed. So we rewarded them,"* said the former SVP of People Operations, Laszlo Bock.

Finally, permission to fail needs to come from the top in the form of leaders admitting their own mistakes. Long-time Lockheed CEO Dan Haughton once famously gathered all his manufacturing heads to share his own mistakes, including his failure to buy a rival company when it was struggling, a bad call that haunted him for years.

OVERCOME FEAR WITH FLOW

When I embark on a new project and the fear – in for the form of a mind busy with chatter and doubts – comes in, my tried and tested method is to get myself into a state of flow as soon as possible. This state of total immersion, of being completely absorbed in a task, is what legendary psychologist Mihaly Csikszentmihalyi termed 'flow'.

We have all been in flow at some time or other. It is a wonderful and highly productive state in which we're so absorbed that time flies. But most importantly, flow sweeps away fear. You have no time for it. Your whole being is involved in what you are doing and there is no space for indulging in fear and 'what ifs?' There is too much positive momentum to stop.

The way to get flow is to start doing something – anything. At BBs you won't often get the chance to get into the flow of innovation because fear freezes you. Inherent in every new thing you do is the real possibility, however small, it won't work out. That's why nothing happens in many BBs. Innovation requires faith in the unknown and it carries with it a risk that the unknown might not work. But if you can starting acting and get in the flow, you kill that fear, creating and open, supportive environment where innovation can happen.

• • •

Goethe's quote about commitment is powerful yet straightforward advice: *"Whatever you can do or dream, begin it."* Overcoming fear is about taking small steps, not embarking on some dramatic transformation. Don't be paralysed by fear of new projects or change; instead, when you feel gripped by fear, just begin. Your momentum will crowd out your fear.

9

DON'T
THINK OF 'NO'
AS A STOP SIGN

**DO
THINK
OF IT AS
A BADGE
OF HONOUR**

Expect and welcome resistance to new ideas

Have you always believed that new ideas will be welcomed with open arms if they're good, and rejected only if they are bad? If so, you are badly mistaken. This is another myth. Whatever we might claim, people in general do not love the new. Our knee-jerk reaction is to resist new things.

Every great idea has been derided, sneered at and flat-out rejected – not once, but multiple times. Scott Burkan offers some memorable examples in his book *The Myths of Innovation.* Take the Eiffel tower, for a start. Many demanded it be torn down when it was first built, calling it a, *"Tragic lamp post springing up... like a beacon of disaster and despair."* And let's not forget that Ken Olsen, founder of Digital Equipment Corporation, claimed in 1977, *"There is no reason anyone would want a computer in their home."*

My own journey through entrepreneurship (and life in general) is, in essence, one long string of rejections. I was rejected three times by the law firm that I ended up working for. My first book, *Anyone Can Do It*, was rejected by ten publishers. Everyone thought coffee bars wouldn't work in the UK, and that we were crazy to leave our professional careers to open one. The first rejections came from family and friends, then from bank managers (*"Bringing coffee to a tea-drinking nation?"* they said. *"Ludicrous!"*), and then suppliers – no one wanted to touch us with a barge pole.

This is nothing compared to the experience of Starbucks CEO Howard Schultz. He racked up 276 'no's from bankers who refused to back his idea of an Italian-style coffee shop in Seattle. Imagine what it felt like to have your idea rejected 276 times – and then imagine what it took to knock on the 277th door.

Even our customers rejected us initially. When we opened our first location, no one came. Our break-even sales were £700, and we made £200 a day. This continued for about six months. Looking at the change on our high streets that's happened since – by 2020 there will be 20,000 coffee bars in the UK – it's easy to imagine that bringing US-style coffee bars to the UK was instantly recognised as a great idea, but that's far from the reality of the experience.

So forget stories of overnight success – almost all of them fail to reveal the true extent of rejection the (ultimately successful) businesses experienced along the way.

This is true for entrepreneurs, but it's also true within BBs. If you are taking forward a new idea in a BB, you will, by definition, collide with an obstacle course, a wall of resistance, just as entrepreneurs do. These 'no's are final. They are probably not what you are used to hearing and, even worse, they carry a stigma of failure. For many in these companies, a rejected idea means a bad idea – it's a black mark on your track record and fear of this stigma can be paralyzing, as we saw in the last section.

In a start-up, it's easy to ignore critics. You just walk away from the naysayers. If one bank manager rejects you, it's on to another. You can cancel out the noise of your friends and family who say, "*This will never work.*" You simply avoid them. You can keep schtum when customers are slow to come round to your product. But in a BB it's different. You can't walk away and say, 'next!' You're working with the same people every day; they're on the inside with you. It's demoralising to have everyone around you undermining and doubting your ideas constantly, watching, judging, criticising and rolling their eyes.

But entrepreneurs know there's no way to innovate without hearing 'no'. Start-up founders expect 'no's from the outset. The fundamental tenet is that, 'If they're not saying 'no', someone's doing it already.' You know you are pushing boundaries – it's implicit in your new title, and in entrepreneurship folklore, that you will meet resistance. So you get used to what I call 'notching up the 'no's'. You almost end up expecting them. It becomes a numbers game – the more 'no's you get, the closer you are to the 'yes'. The repetitive nature of reacting to these 'no's means our persistence muscles get pretty strong and well-developed.

But it's different when you're working at a BB. If progressing in your career is about avoiding rejection and never hearing a 'no', what's the point in persistence? This goes back to the fear of failure we discussed earlier: the fear of people saying no is a big part of that fear. So, unless you change your attitude to hearing 'no' and meeting resistance, you will never try new things and you'll return constantly to the status quo – same old, same old. There's no way to innovate without experiencing rejection, so whenever you kick-start a new idea, aim to notch up 'no's, knowing that the more times you hear 'no', the closer you get to hearing 'yes'.

How do you notch up 'no's without losing your enthusiasm for fresh ideas? This is a question I always get asked from audiences inside BBs. How did we manage not to give up at the tenth or twentieth or thirty-ninth rejection? Here are some concrete actions that can help you get better at weathering rejection.

ACTIONS

KEEP IT UNDER THE RADAR

We've talked about protecting ugly babies, trying small experiments and keeping budgets small. The idea behind all three is that if you don't have to get authorisation, you can avoid what is called 'corporate immune response' – the instinctive reflex to attack and destroy anything new and different. This way, by the time you do attract attention, your idea is not just abstract concept but has some traction.

CHANGE HOW YOU THINK ABOUT REJECTION

The main thing is to stop thinking of 'no' as a stopping point or a warning sign of career failure. Instead, start thinking of rejection as an essential part of creativity. Rejection is a sign you're on the right track – not only is your idea new and interesting enough to merit a 'no' from the unimaginative, but notching up 'no's also proves you're acting on your idea, not just dreaming about it. It's a numbers game – the more you try (as we saw in section six, James Dyson made 5,127 versions of his Cyclone Vacuum cleaner), the more likely you are to succeed.

Also, remember that 'no' is not necessarily a judgment on your work. Saying 'no' is simply easier than saying 'yes'. Coasting along, accepting the status quo, keeping things as they are, is much easier than exploring the merits of a new idea. It's the safe way. When you hear 'no', remind yourself that the response is quite probably a reflection of the speaker's mentality – or their mood – and not of your idea.

You've spent countless hours researching and perfecting your idea, convincing yourself of its merits. How long has your colleague had with it? Maybe five minutes? Just because this person says 'no', does it mean you have to abandon it? No-one is likely to be as interested in your idea as you are; this doesn't mean you shouldn't pursue it.

BAN ANY FORM OF EYE-ROLLING

Sometimes it's not a simple 'no' you hear. Instead, 'no' comes disguised as cynicism, as a sneer. The effects of this is detrimental. Former Tesco boss Sir Terry Leahy talks about how the culture he built was vigilant even about eye-rolls, and about what a huge impact they have on free-spirited thinking. It goes back to fear of failure. If you're paying attention to something as subtle as an eye roll then, as leader, you are removing the fear of judgement when someone suggests something different. You're keeping the culture receptive and stimulating curiosity – which we know is vital for innovation.

Pixar does this with a technique called 'plussing'. The rule is that you may only criticise an idea if you add a constructive suggestion – a new idea for strengthening the original concept. Hence the name 'plussing' – always adding something, never subtracting enthusiasm. It's a technique that comes from improvisational comedy, where 'yes, and…' is used to build a scene and create a story, rather than 'yes, but…', which brings the story to an abrupt halt. The 'How might we…' technique I discuss in section five does something similar.

• • •

Hopefully, viewing rejection in this way will give you the resilience to withstand the barrage of 'No's' that is part and parcel of bringing any new idea to life. History is full of people who gave up on good ideas too early. If you can learn to push through, proudly notching up resistance and rejection as you go, you won't be among them.

10

DON'T
PUT A WORK
FACE ON

**DO
BE 100%
YOURSELF**

Creating a more human work culture is the easiest, most natural thing to do

Sometime in the early nineties, working at a dry-as-dust law firm, I disconsolately asked my colleague why we had so little fun. "*They're not paying you to enjoy yourself*," she answered, fixing me with a flinty stare.

At that time, the words 'fun' and 'work' were polar opposites. You left your real self at the door and put on your 'work face' when you walked into the building. You reconnected with the real, 'whole' you when you left, and fun was certainly restricted to out-of-work hours (or maybe the Christmas party). That's why work-life balance was such a hot topic of the day. It implied that 'work' and 'life' were separate and opposite.

For me, at the time, entrepreneurship was the solution. By leaving the conventional work world to start a business, I could be 100% myself at work. That's what used to distinguish entrepreneurs from employees. The price for the salary and security of steady employment was the 'low freedom' culture that demanded conformity and uniformity. Start-ups, on the other hand, were 'high freedom'. The reward for the risk and uncertainty were all the perks that freedom brings.

But all this is changing. The world outside has shifted dramatically and so, correspondingly, the culture inside BBs must change. 'Low freedom' doesn't work anymore. It is inconsistent with the external world of digital connection. Micromanaging people like machines produces exactly that, automatons. Automatons worked in the old world where change was slow, proven business models were permanent, and success was just a matter of executing them. The trouble is, in our new world, which demands empathy, agility, and a sense of ownership and purpose, automatons are the last thing you need. The uniformity that BBs used to prize so greatly as a precursor to productivity is a creativity killer.

Automatons can't empathise with customers. Automatons aren't curious. Automatons can't experiment or be passionate. Leaving your personal life out of your professional life creates a joyless existence, and the new generation of workers aren't wired for working that way. They will run for the hills in a culture that doesn't allow them to be 100% themselves. BBs can't afford to lose them. Diversity and inclusion are not politically correct buzzwords any more. They are a strategic imperative.

All of this is great news for people in BBs who might have been envying the freedom, the fun, the individuality of entrepreneurs. This new culture gives you the upsides of entrepreneurship within a BB.

Of course, it's not so easy to change a culture that has become entrenched. The militaristic legacy of a command and control has been there for a very long time. It's easy to look at Silicon Valley and assume that the key to creating a culture of freedom is just to introduce scooters in the office, install a foosball table and stock up on free gourmet snacks. Those things are fine if you want to offer them, but they are actually distractions from the true shift that's required. Changing your culture to one that not only permits, but actually encourages fun is simpler (if more difficult to execute) than introducing a bunch of 'fun' perks.

It might sound too obvious but changing a stuck-in-the-past culture is simply about bringing the human element back to an organisation made up of, well, humans.

The reason you can be 100% yourself at start-ups is because you can't *not* be. Like all other 'lacks' that might appear at first to be weaknesses in a start-up (lack of bureaucracy, lack of expertise, lack of resources), the fact that a start-up has nothing else to fall back on, no systems or processes, means it has to rely on its people – their drive, their tenacity and their vision. Their heads, their hearts and their souls must be completely engaged. In a start-up, it's all in.

In a BB, of course they say people matter, just like they say 'the customer is king' (see Shift #1), but it's not like a start-up where people are truly everything. In a start-up people are the engine. In a BB it's the bureaucracy that drives things. The foolproof systems and processes in place to safeguard the current business override the power of individuals. The old world was slow to change, and success didn't need empowered individuals. It needed cogs in a machine producing consistent results.

This new model, where innovation is a daily activity, does need empowered individuals. And you can't feel empowered if you are micromanaged. It's human nature. In arenas from politics to preschool, we intuitively understand this simple human law: if you trust people, you bring out their best because they feel empowered.

If you don't believe me, think back to your own childhood. Which teacher empowered you more, the one taking attendance registers, assigning seats, and watching over your shoulder, or the one that let you know they believed in you? In which type of class did you do your best work? Monitoring people infantilises rather than empowers them.

Of course, it's easy to establish the right culture in a start-up. At Coffee Republic, we personally were the culture and everyone who joined got infused with that culture by close proximity to us, by osmosis almost. But changing an entrenched culture at a BB isn't as hard as it seems at first. Others have managed it. So can your organisation.

ACTIONS

A HUMAN WORK CULTURE NEEDS TRUST

If the opposite of command and control culture is a 'high freedom' culture, then what is the prerequisite of freedom? The incredibly simple answer is trust. If you trust people, you give them freedom. If you don't, you micromanage them.

The best example of a culture based on trust I've seen is L'Oréal, whose culture reinforces their belief in individuals. *"L'Oréal is not like other companies that say, 'Our people are our best assets'. That's not what we mean. What we mean is a fundamental belief that individuals make a difference. Not processes, not systems, not committees, but a person with a first name and a last name,"* Michel Brousset, then MD of L'Oréal UK told me. Everything they do, from flexible working, to not punishing failure, reinforces their belief in individuals.

Or you can use Google as a template. In his book, *Work Rules!*, the company's former HR boss Laszlo Bock outlines the many ways Google has created a 'high freedom culture'. It involves largely leaving employees to decide when and how to work, and sharply limiting the power of supervisors to micromanage their teams. This might sound like a radical idea, but the thinking behind it is dead simple. *"When we feel free, we do our best work,"* Bock has explained.

Ariel Eckstein, a VP at LinkedIn, gives a short and sweet description of their trusting culture: *"Rather than seventeen pages on flexible working arrangements we ask, 'What do you need to do your job well?'"*

At the furthest end of the spectrum, Netflix, which also has a culture of 'freedom and responsibility', declares that because it hires only 'fully-formed adults', it treats employees as such, allowing them to take unlimited vacation and claim expenses without approval from their managers. Netflix makes up for the lack of structure by holding their people to very high standards of performance. They don't measure face time; they measure results.

The Netflix model may be too extreme for many, but its essence can act as an inspiration for any business. Removing the guardrails of micromanagement might seem frightening, but there is no denying human nature: when we feel trusted and are treated like "fully-formed adults" we rise to the occassion. In the words of Lazlo Bock, give employees freedom and "they will surprise, delight and amaze you".

A HUMAN WORK CULTURE NEEDS FUN

'Fun' at work is definitely a touchy subject for many people I have worked with. It was sneered at, for example, by a risk group in a financial services firm I spoke with. Actuaries can't have 'fun', they told me. But I don't mean the 'dancing on a float at the Rio carnival with a fruit bowl on your head' sort of fun. When I say 'fun', all I mean is reconnecting with the human element of your colleagues so work becomes human to human rather than de-personalised and emotionally sterile. Michael Brousset says collaboration happens through *"friendships, not through distant layers of hierarchy[...] When you are amongst friends, people listen."*

How do you reintroduce this human connection to teams, like those sceptical actuaries I met, that haven't traditionally had it? LinkedIn CEO Jeff Weiner has new hires participate in mini talent competitions to introduce them to the team. What better way to break the ice than a talent competition where loss of face is very likely? Brent Smart, CEO of Saatchi & Saatchi NY, hosts monthly 'Family Dinners' where a diverse group of people from around the company gather to chat and bond. These events are rumored to sometimes end with karaoke over dessert.

If you hate singing, you can plan a different sort of get together. The point isn't any particular event or activity, it's providing some sort of opportunity for colleagues to get to know each other as full, complete humans. The impetus driving initiatives like these isn't 'fun' on a surface level. Nor are the best of them simply boss-mandated fake fun. These gatherings are worth doing because they help people remove their masks and be themselves at work, vulnerabilities and all. And being truly, fully human in this way helps them do better, more creative work.

A HUMAN WORK CULTURE NEEDS PURPOSE

All the fun and bonding suggested in the examples above would be empty and shallow unless people also feel a sense of purpose. Purpose doesn't have to be some grand, saving the world sort of purpose. Purpose, for me, means two things. First, who you are is aligned with what you do, so that what you do suits your personality and your interests and plays to your strengths. And second, that you understand the meaning of what you do every day at work.

I know many people in BBs struggle with the word 'purpose'. They feel they can't find purpose in the dry world of less 'worthy' businesses. But this feeling comes from the myth that purpose means grand undertakings like curing disease or saving the planet. I think purpose can come from something as simple as seeing the effect of what you do on the end recipient – on a fellow human. Purpose is built on empathy and comes from seeing that you are actually making a difference, even if that just means you provide someone with a better cup of coffee. Even if you have only internal customers, seeing the effect of what you do for your customers' customers can give meaning to your work.

Adam Grant, in his book *Give or Take*, tells of startling study of employees at a university's fundraising call centre. By far the most productive employees were those who had read stories from the recipients of scholarships funded by their efforts about how the scholarships changed their lives. When another group of employees actually met scholarship students to hear their stories in person, fundraising went up by 400%.

Given these incredible numbers, it's shocking how many companies don't give everyone – not just customer-facing employees – the powerful motivation of seeing close up what a difference their work makes to customers This creates empathy, as I discussed at the start of this book, but it also feeds purpose, which in turn boosts engagement and empathy. Impacting lives gives you purpose which drives you to impact more lives, and so on. It's a powerful positive feedback loop. It's also a lot of fun.

A HUMAN WORK CULTURE NEEDS ALIGNMENT

Purpose isn't just feeling that what you do makes a difference. It's also feeling that your work and your personal strengths are aligned. By a certain stage in life we all know what we like doing, what we hate doing, what we are good at and what we are not good at. And we all want to feel our work plays to those preferences and strengths.

As Brazilian CEO Ricardo Semler points out in his wonderful book *Maverick*, a mission or calling isn't only for scientists, surgeons and ministers. *"Everyone has a wealth of instincts, interests and skills that combine to form their talents. Some refer to it as a 'calling',"* he says, and, *"The best way to ensure job satisfaction in the long run is to exhaust that reservoir."*

My own rule of thumb is: if you are enjoying yourself and good at it, then you are 'exhausting that reservoir'. Or if you prefer loftier language, you have found your calling. If you hate your work, you are in the wrong job – maybe not the wrong company, but perhaps the wrong team or role. You might even need to take a step "down" to regain your sense of purpose. It's surprising how much our promotions and 'successes' can lead us away from our calling. I've met many sales people who have sales running through their veins and yet they get promoted to a position remote from any selling and end up miserable and lost.

Part of being 100% yourself at work is having open and honest conversations with your team or supervisor if you feel elements of your position or responsibilities have veered away from your strengths and interests. There is always a solution, and it's in both you and your company's interests to find a way to get you re-aligned with what you do.

In the words of Henry Ford, *"A man who does not get a certain satisfaction out of his day's work is losing the best part of his pay."* Life is far too short not to be true to ourselves in what we do most of our waking hours for the best years of our lives.

● ● ●

All the shifts I outline in this book, from leaning into empathy to encouraging experimentation and curiosity are all, at base, about embracing Ford's essential wisdom. Business success and happiness at work are not at cross-purposes to each other. Employees do their best work when they feel trusted and empowered to use their full selves to make a real difference. Human-friendly workplaces make people happy, but they also make businesses successful.

That's why I truly believe that hidden in the massive challenges facing organisations lies a golden opportunity. You could think of the sunset of old ways of doing business as a scary and uncomfortable disruption, or you can see this change as an opportunity to transform work into a place employees actually want to come to every day, a place that brings out their best and uses their talents to the maximum. You could use this moment to make your organisation not just far more successful, but far more human.

Talk about a silver lining.

ACKNOWLEDGEMENTS

This book is my first experience in the unchartered world of self- publishing so I owe some big thank you's:

Jessica Stillman, who applies her magic writing skills and transforms a half-baked sentence to exactly what I intended it to be. Jason Dunne for sharing so generously his deep knowledge and contacts in the publishing world. Brendan O Connor for encouraging me to leap into this new form of publishing and the (much needed) guiding . Victoria Roddam for re-looking at this manuscript and bringing freshness when I could no longer see the words. Sophie Burdess for her immense creativity for the cover design and styling. Jeff Scott at Platypus PR for his out-of-the-box thinking and immense dedication and for introducing me to Vicky Holtham at Sitting Duck for typesetting and all sorts of marketing help. And finally the team at Matador for bearing with me for being a stickler for every little detail.

And finally I am so grateful for my career as a speaker which has opened up a whole new world to me; so big thank you goes to the companies that invite me and my speaker agents who make it all happen. I hope this book is as useful and applicable as I intend it to be.

ABOUT THE AUTHOR

Sahar Hashemi left her career as a lawyer in London to start the UK's first coffee bar chain, Coffee Republic with her brother, Bobby, which became one of the most recognized high street brands with a turnover of £30m. Sahar left the business in 2001 and wrote the bestselling book, *Anyone Can Do It: Building Coffee Republic from our Kitchen Table.* In 2005 she founded a sugar free sweets brand, Skinny Candy, which was sold two years later to confectionary conglomerate Glisten PLC.

In the decades since, Sahar has become recognized as the leading industry expert on entrepreneurship in the corporate world, and has spoken to – or worked with – over 400 companies. She has been selected as a Young Global Leader by the World Economic Forum, named as a Pioneer to the Life of the Nation by the Queen and was nominated by *Director* magazine as one of its Top 10 Original Thinkers. In 2012 she was awarded OBE (Officer of the British Empire) for services to the UK economy and to charity.

She is currently co- chair of the Government Scale Up Taskforce and is actively involved in the roll-out of Change Please, a social enterprise that trains and hires homeless people to run coffee carts.